CONTROLLED CHAOS

Surgical Adventures in
Chitokoloki Mission Hospital

CHITOKOLOKI MISSION

1914 - 2014

Royalties from the sale of this book will be donated to the work
of the Chitokoloki Mission Hospital.

There is a web page for the book located at
www.davidgalloway.co.uk
and full colour versions of the images used in the book
can be found there.

CONTROLLED CHAOS

Surgical Adventures in Chitokoloki Mission Hospital

David Galloway
with Jenni Galloway

RITCHIE
John Ritchie Publishing

40 Beansburn, Kilmarnock, Scotland

ISBN-13: 978 1 912522 88 0

Copyright © 2020 by John Ritchie Ltd.
40 Beansburn, Kilmarnock, Scotland

www.ritchiechristianmedia.co.uk

Typeset by John Ritchie Ltd., Kilmarnock
Printed by Bell & Bain Ltd., Glasgow

Dedication

For my wife Christine, for her continuing love and support.

For Lynda who worries about us when we are away and for Sat who has experienced African missionary life and knows exactly what it is like.

For Jaz (8), Isla (6) and Anya (3), that they would grow up to develop a strong Christian faith for themselves and enjoy reading some of these tales in the years ahead.

Acknowledgements

I am grateful for the amazing, committed and dedicated example set by many of the long-term mission partners in Chitokoloki. In particular, David and Lorraine McAdam and Julie-Rachel Elwood were happy to patiently guide and redirect the views and attitudes that I had honed in Western clinical practice and remodel these to the reality of patient care in a remote rural African Mission Hospital. I was shown nothing but kindness, support and wonderful hospitality by David and Lorraine and also by Gordon and Ruth Hanna, Joey and Kaitlin Speichinger, Dorothy Woodside, Shawn and Rhonda Markle, Chris and Alison Brundage and Steven and Hannah Wallace. It was also wonderful to have the support of my colleague, Dr Ros Jefferson, who not only provided unstinting paediatric care at all hours of the day and night but who was also a bundle of energy, great company and wonderful hostess with an uncanny ability to concoct gourmet meals for large groups with little apparent difficulty!

I am grateful to my friend and colleague Jonathan Hannay, also a frequent visitor to Chit, for writing the Foreward.

I am also very grateful for the interest and support from the staff of John Ritchie Ltd and I would particularly like to thank Alison Banks for her enthusiasm and guidance and Fraser Munro for his editing advice.

Finally to my wife, Christine, who has always shown real support for these (sometimes) prolonged trips away from home. I would love her to come to Africa with me but the threat of various "beasties" has moderated any enthusiasm she might have entertained.

David Galloway
May 2020

Endorsements

David Galloway provides a vivid picture of the immense challenges, joys and sorrows of medical and surgical practice in remote rural Africa. This book may not be for the faint-hearted or squeamish, nevertheless the presentation of the range of diseases, seen at an advanced stage by medical health professionals on a daily basis, shows the huge gap that still exists between medical care in the West and the Majority World. You will definitely be stirred as you read of the contribution made by committed and courageous Christian workers in Central Africa.

Dr Ian Burness,
Former General Director, Echoes of Service,
Author of 'From Glasgow to Garanganze:
Frederick Stanley Arnot and Nineteenth-Century African Mission'

I loved reading this book. The sights, the sounds, the smells … these memoirs took me on a tantalising journey right back to where I experienced the same laughter, tears, sadness, joy and hope at Chitokoloki in 2014. David and Jenni's frank, sincere and yet humorous approach reflects well the modus operandi at Chit. It is an incredible place, where pragmatism, perseverance and a desire to share God's loving-kindness power the hardest-working and most self-sacrificial team I've ever met.

Dr Rachel McLatchie
Emergency Medicine Trainee,
South East Scotland.

As I was reading this book several questions kept coming into my mind: What if the hospital wasn't there? What if there were no trained and utterly dedicated doctors and nurses there? What would happen to all these people desperately needing such a wide variety of treatments? We are deeply indebted to the author who has given us a unique insight into what really goes on in a mission hospital. The sacrifice of the medical personnel as they strive under unbelievably difficult conditions to bring healing, both physical and spiritual, to the people God has called them to serve, is an engrossing and challenging read.

Derek Malcolm,
Publisher, Middle East.

An amazing account of 21st Century mission, which has as its focus, people. People helped, healed, and given new hope. People, using their time and skills, serving others with the compassion of Christ. A pilot, a paediatric neurologist, a construction specialist, nurses, a final year student, an abdominal surgeon, an 18-year old maintenance worker and a pathologist, contributing from a distance. My prayer for this book is exactly as the author hopes, 'That this account might inspire others to help in whatever way they can.' People, being mobilised, to take the Gospel to the nations.

John Aitken,
General Director, Echoes International.

It is with enormous enthusiasm that I commend this account, by one of Scotland's most distinguished surgeons, of daily life in a busy mission hospital in rural Zambia. Like me, you will be moved by the needs of so many disadvantaged people, and inspired by the incredible devotion and skill of the hospital staff, both permanent and visiting, as in this challenging context they seek to demonstrate the love of God and share the Christian Gospel. I wish this remarkable record of modern missionary endeavour a wide readership.

Very Rev Dr Angus Morrison
Chaplain in Scotland to HM the Queen

Contents

Preface

This book brings together a real life account of day to day activity in a Mission Hospital in rural Africa. I have had the opportunity to visit Chitokoloki in the North Western Province of Zambia several times over a period of five years, spending a month or two each time. Why? Well, I have always had an interest in medical missions, but having spent a career serving as an academic Consultant Surgeon in the NHS I really did wonder whether my skill set and experience would be of any real value in the African bush. Having been aware of Chitokoloki Mission Hospital, I made contact with Dr. David McAdam, a surgical colleague who has been based there for many years. Would my narrow specialist practice and experience of high tech medicine and minimal access (so-called keyhole) surgery be applicable there? What about having to work in a setting with severely limited resources? Would I be able to cope – or contribute? It seemed sensible to speak to David. His clinical experience and expertise is quite unlike any other colleague I have ever encountered. Working single-handedly for most of the time means that he not only has to look after patients with diverse problems that would be distributed to a range of other specialists in the West, he also has to keep up to date, maintain records, bear the burden of teaching, and administration, not to mention being available 24 hours a day 7 days a week! He has prepared well for solitary medical practice in a remote setting by training in surgery and anaesthetics as well as obstetrics. Working alone for many years he has had to be capable of dealing with conditions and clinical challenges that cross specialty boundaries and the result is expertise in an astonishing array of disciplines such as surgery (every branch), obstetrics and gynaecology, ophthalmology, paediatrics, intensive care, anaesthetics – the list goes on. There are other colleagues who help out with complex orthopaedics and plastic surgery on an occasional basis. As well as providing expert, Western style medical care David carries the additional responsibility of sharing his Christian convictions as a medical missionary. In addition to the demanding medical work, he is committed to helping people explore and understand the Bible in order to deepen their personal experience of God. As a result he is regularly called upon to lead Bible studies, preach and teach in the local church and in the surrounding communities. 'Remarkable' fails to adequately cover it!

"David, do you think I could be of any help to you? I know virtually nothing about tropical medicine and, like every other surgeon in the UK, my surgical practice has become progressively narrower over the past twenty years." For him, it seemed to come down to a fairly simple matter. "If you can operate, we can certainly use you here."

On the strength of that and still plagued by a measure of uncertainty and apprehension, I made arrangements to go to Chitokoloki for two months in the autumn of 2015. Quite unable to persuade my wife that it might be a good idea for her to accompany me; she cited teaching duties at home but in reality I realised that the prospect of having to cope with creepy crawlies and other forms of reptilian life clinched and confirmed the decision in her mind.

The stories and reflections I share here are a personal selection drawn from notes that I recorded at the end of each day. Most of the short chapters or sections represent a summary of a single day. The actual dates are not especially important but I have left a few details to anchor the accounts in time in order to provide some context.

I wanted to try to capture the detail of these patients and their circumstances and to convey the sometimes almost unbelievable reality that their experience represents. When I started to make these observations they were prepared as a kind of daily news blog for the consumption of my family back in the UK but, as is the nature of digital media these days, they found their way around many friends and even did the rounds amongst members of my local golf club. Again and again, they have been the focus of discussion and enquiry and it has been good to share the experience to the point that others who become aware are ready to pray, support, give and even visit in order to contribute in some way to the work of the mission. I welcome the opportunity to offer this account even although it provides a tiny sample of the experience of those working there full time. It would be wonderful if even some of their many stories could be written down and passed on but I fear that the full time mission staff are just too stretched in dealing with the demanding issues of providing care and support in the hospital, church and around the community that the best of these amazing experiences may never make it into print. This, therefore, comes from a daily stream of the business of living and working in a remote mission hospital and taken together amounts to a total of around six months' experience spread over five visits (2015-2019).

My daughter Jenni who is an Emergency Medicine specialist trainee accompanied me on my second trip to Chitokoloki. She had previously spent two months in Chit as her medical student elective. I have included her account of the visit we shared – for each of us our second experience although the fun part was that we were able to go together and even work as a team. You can read her personal and amusing review on pages 115-137.

My hope is that this book will provide an accurate account of the reality of medical missionary endeavour in the African bush. It's all here; abject suffering in a resource poor setting, staff from many different countries working alongside dedicated Zambians, stories of individual patients and their many and various problems and a commentary on observed aspects of life for a beautiful and cheerful people who have more than their fair share of difficulties. Sometimes the medical work is frustrating simply because conditions which would be readily treated in the developed world are just not manageable in remote parts of Africa. Indeed, the provision of medical and surgical care on the global scene has become an extremely hot topic and many health care professionals now devote a great deal of energy and ingenuity to try to improve prospects for African patients. Beyond the service provision, a number of global agencies like the World Health Organisation as well as individual medical colleges and universities in the US, the UK and Australasia have become active in addressing the desperate need for medical and surgical support from both a policy and practical point of view.

It has been a very significant privilege to participate in some small way to provide assistance and encouragement to friends who work in Chitokoloki year round. What they provide is unstinting care. 'Above and beyond' takes on a new meaning.

Foreword

"Ping!!!" announced my phone in the dark as I lay sweltering under my mosquito net in the sub-tropical heat. It was a text from David Galloway. "Johnny, where are you?" it read.

"I'm currently in Tanzania helping pilot a medical training course. Where are you?" I replied.

"At Chitokoloki in Zambia visiting David McAdam. You really need to get yourself out here..."

That initially surreal but now surprisingly modern experience of having a real-time text-conversation while in remote regions of the world has stayed with me - as has David's keen interest in the work at Chitokoloki.

In your hands now is a book of David's reflections from his years of visiting Chitokoloki Mission Hospital in North-Western Zambia from 2015 through to the present. Being a surgeon, David's stories naturally gravitate to surgical care in the chaos that a mission hospital tries to bring to sense and order. As anyone who has visited Chitokoloki, or any other similar mission hospital, can attest, the medical stories told are not rare 'cases' curated for "wow!" factor but are genuinely typical stories of people who daily come through the doors of a mission hospital in desperate need of help and compassionate care. Making sense in the chaos, therefore, requires more than expert use of a scalpel, or the seemingly indefatigable resilience shown by the long-term workers, but a pastoral heart that tends to the spirit, soul, and body of those in need. The quote attributed to Sir William Osler is most germane: "The good physician treats the disease; the great physician treats the patient who has the disease" and David shows how this is borne out at Chitokoloki.

Further to the interest factor in the work at the mission hospital at Chit, David's very real and personal writing gives a perspective rarely encountered in books and reports of mission-related work in foreign lands: that of the regular, repeat short-term volunteer. This additionally makes the book valuable since it speaks to a growing demographic in our modern times and attests to the experiences that those in that demographic share. These experiences, with reflection, are different from those of the 'single-trip' volunteer or the missionary with years of service in a single culture - each of which has something valuable to say too!

Approximately twenty-five years ago I approached David for advice about volunteering and spending some time at a mission hospital. He listened patiently, nodded, and wisely said: "I advise you to get some more experience first..." so I count it a real privilege to write this foreword to David's own experiences and commend it to you in the warmest terms possible for your own reflection and blessing.

Jonathan Hannay
Consultant Surgeon
General and Colorectal Surgery
Inverclyde Royal Hospital
Greenock,
Scotland.

Africa – for the first time

Sparkling waters

I had been interested in becoming involved in surgical care in Africa for many years but in the midst of a busy clinical and academic career in the UK the time never did seem quite right. Eventually, I made email contact with Dr David McAdam. David is a most remarkable character. He has served as a missionary surgeon in rural Africa (both in what is now the Democratic Republic of Congo and latterly in the Republic of Zambia) for close to 30 years. He and his family have paid a heavy price. On at least two occasions they have lost all their possessions, once as a result of a catastrophe involving the transportation of all their goods, belongings, textbooks and so on. On the other occasion, the damage was the result of tribal violence as the hospital they had established, equipped and built-up was ransacked and looted by rebels who wantonly and thoughtlessly destroyed everything in their path. I had to express my misgivings and admit that having practised surgery as a consultant in a major teaching hospital in Scotland, I did not feel well placed to deal with the kind of patients, conditions and circumstances with which I would have to contend in Zambia. David seemed quite relaxed about my lack of preparation and predicted that I would be of some value so I filed away the intention of making my way out to join him and hopefully learn the ropes.

As it happened, my younger daughter, Jenni, was a medical student in Aberdeen at about that time and seized the opportunity to do one of her elective attachments with Dr McAdam. She had the opportunity to get to Zambia before I could and when she arrived on the mission station I quickly received her initial reaction in a text message. "Dad, this place is mental! You have to get out here!"

Zambia is a young nation in the midst of south central Africa. Like many nations within the African continent, it is massive, just over 290,000 square miles. It became independent of colonial administration in 1964 under the presidency of Kenneth Kaunda. The early years following independence were characterised by economic challenges, political turmoil and numerous tense exchanges with surrounding nations. The population is expanding fast and at the time of the last census there were some 16.5 million souls living in the country. From an economic point of view, there are vast mineral resources and active mining continues for copper, nickel, tin and uranium. The decline in value of copper in the 1970s led to significant national debt but a measure of recovery together with inward investment from overseas has contributed to a much more stable economic scenario. Zambia is a nominally Christian nation and while around a fifth of the population is Roman Catholic some 75% are identified with a protestant group of some description. There are particular health challenges in the country. The infant and maternal mortality rates are high; HIV / AIDS continues to be a significant problem with some 12.5% of the population infected and while good quality medical and surgical provision is improving and there is a coherent national surgical plan, the reality is that a large proportion of the rural population have no integrated health service and standard hospital emergency care is simply unavailable. It is a striking example of the stark detail exposed by the Lancet Commission on Global Surgery indicating that worldwide, some 5 billion people cannot access timely, safe and effective medical and surgical care when needed.[1]

Chitokoloki – the name means 'sparkling waters,' is a settlement in the North Western corner of Zambia. The Mission Station has been active since 1914 at which time three pioneering missionaries[2], including Frederick Stanley Arnot from Glasgow, identified the site and laid the foundations for the hub of activity that exists today. David Livingstone had inspired Arnot and in fact Livingstone's family were near neighbours as Arnot was growing up and this undoubtedly had a major effect on Arnot's life.

The nearest provincial town to Chitokoloki is Zambezi which is just over 40km away. At least half of the journey to town involves bumping along a very rough sandy track before reaching a road with a prepared tar surface. Zambezi is a bustling town but it is still remote and it far from boasts the benefits associated with modern urban civilisation.

The Mission Station has several hospital buildings together with housing for the local missionaries as well as staff houses and some guest accommodation. The mission is elevated on a plain overlooking the banks of the mighty river Zambezi. The landscape is otherwise flat as far as the eye can see. The Zambezi cuts a slash running north to south and is fringed with brush connecting to the local community by means of a network of sandy tracks leading from the villages to the riverside. There are large flat expanses close to the river and there are always people moving around. On one part of the local flood plain there is a small lake adjacent to a flat patch of rough ground. Such is the enthusiasm for football that the local team have erected two sets of goalposts and marked out the indistinct boundaries of a football pitch. It turns out that this is a favoured site for training and practice with the occasional match taking place there. Some of these contests are keenly fought despite the lack of equipment and it is hard not to be impressed by the enthusiasm and fitness of the players. There is little evidence of football colours although you will see the occasional participant sporting a ragged English premiership top. Football boots appear to be optional and are used by around half of the players – even in competitive matches. The area appears fertile although formal signs of cultivation are more difficult to recognise. On the mission station there are also two schools (grades 1-12), an airstrip and hangar, a large well-equipped maintenance facility, a church building and even a swimming pool.

There are many elements of living and working in rural Africa that are culturally so different from Western civilisation. As far as the medical work is concerned, several distinctive factors sharply contrast to any other hospital in which I have worked. The entire ethos in Chitokoloki is based around medical mission; a desire to communicate the importance of faith in Christ and a demonstration of Christian love through the provision of free medical care. The full-time mission workers at Chitokoloki[3] are driven by the desire to demonstrate God's love for people by investing their time, energy and resources. I am full of admiration for the permanent mission workers, who sacrifice the opportunity to have a lucrative and comfortable career in the West to serve where they are so needed. Within the hospital, an important and practical way in which this ethos is manifest is that we pray with each patient before they go under anaesthetic. Imagine that happening in the NHS! There would be a secular outcry. In Zambia, that practice and the attitude that underpins it are deeply appreciated and valued by the local people, especially when they find themselves at one of the most vulnerable times of their lives.

These features help to make this place and the greater endeavour so valuable. There is a bigger picture in view at Chitokoloki, one that transcends the limited secularism that has become typical in the Western world. This is the demonstration of genuine Christian love in practical action.

This is Africa!

Thursday 10th September 2015 was the date of my first arrival in Sub-Saharan Africa. I had travelled extensively in India, Sri Lanka, the Far East and beyond but Africa was quite unlike any of these experiences.

I arrived in Lusaka on schedule from Glasgow, laden with a large bag full of surgical staplers and clinical supplies. I was concerned that my baggage, especially the bag with all the surgical instrumentation would not have made it. There were two reasons; first it was set aside in Glasgow for additional screening and "if there is anything resembling a firearm it will be put aside and you may be challenged at the gate." There was no challenge so my assumption was that it was considered safe. The second potential problem was a pretty short turn around time between my connecting flights in Dubai and thus a real risk that the bags would have been stranded.

On arrival at Lusaka, first there seemed to be a problem with getting an external power supply to the aircraft ('it wasn't working today') so we had to wait a while before getting down the jetway. The temperature was about 32 degrees with a strong dry wind so not unpleasant at all. Typical of an arrival into Lusaka, one has to walk about 300 yards across the apron to the terminal building and then queue for 35 minutes at passport control. I was relieved of $50 for a visa for 30 days. The young girl was pleasant enough – a trifle sullen but I probably wasn't very affable at that point either, having been waiting and all the while looking past the passport control gates at the baggage carousel doing lap after lap and failing to see my two bags. Dozens of bags going round and round and none that looked anything like the ones I had checked in. I had concluded that since the plane from Dubai was just about to leave for Harare there were no more bags to unload; I was resigned to having all my stuff somewhere, but not here! I was mentally preparing a list of the emergency supplies I might need, given that there is not likely any shopping opportunity in the bush. What a pain!

I passed through the turnstile and, behold, both my bags lying unattended having been lifted off the carousel. What a relief to see my distinctive multi-coloured luggage straps and the bags intact. I headed out through the green lane with all my surgical kit and made for the bank in the airport. There was an enormous queue so I went hunting for an ATM and withdrew 1000 kwacha. Just at that point there was a Livingstonian moment when a Canadian voice over my left shoulder said: "Are you Dr. Galloway?" Chris the pilot from Chitokoloki had arrived from Canada earlier that day. What a bonus. Jenni had told me to draw out about £300 worth of Zambian currency. A thousand kwacha is about £66 so I figured I would be short. Chris advised that what I had would be more than enough since there is nothing to spend it on at Chitokoloki anyway!

We went to the Guest House operated by Mission Flight Services, Zambia[4], checked in, met our hosts Crysinthia and Cornwell, ordered our eggs for the morning and then left for a shopping expedition. The last contact with fast food for a while comprised a chicken burger at the Hungry Lion - a slowish fast food stop in a local mall. Then we went shopping for long-life milk and some fresh supplies in Shoprite, a bit like Asda with an African slant. The following day was eventful to say the least.

Instant obstetrics
We said our 'goodbyes' at the Flight House around 7am, loaded

the truck and headed for the airport. The man at the hanger was apologetic about bird poop on the spinner and dust on the aircraft. Chris did the walk around, had a look at the newly-installed engine, did a little tinkering and then loaded up. We taxied across the apron to refuel then we went inside to the terminal building from the runway. Chris then remembered that I would have to pay a departure tax (160 kwacha) so we went to the booth. In typical African style, it was closed and the man with the key had gone! There is even a book with that title written by a medical missionary[5] - it is such a characteristic feature of life in Africa. 'The man with the key has gone.' No one knew where he was but he did materialise after about 20 minutes.

We took off from Runway 08 at Kenneth Kaunda International Airport heading north west to Chitokoloki with a strong tail wind and very hazy flying conditions. The flight took some three hours and everything appeared to be very hot and dry.

As we came in to land at Chitokoloki we seemed to float along the westerly runway without touching down! 'Cool as you like Chris' performed a 'go around' - landing aborted, full power back on, ease back on the controls and re-position over the airfield to look more closely at the windsock. He then tried a landing from

the opposite direction - no problem. We arrived to quite a party of spectators including the Hannas, McAdams, Emma and Christina (two Canadian nurses), Kaitlin (American nurse) and a large number of local people who were curious to watch all the activity.

Having unloaded, I was taken to a nice house, a large two bedroom flat called 'the duplex'. Chris lived in one half and I was given the other. Both the pantry and fridge were fully stocked, including muffins and freshly baked bread. The hospitality in Chitokoloki is outstanding. It was great to meet Gordon and Ruth Hanna for lunch. They came out to Chitokoloki for 6 weeks some thirty years ago! I spent the rest of the afternoon in the clinic seeing all manner of weird and wonderful cases. A few had nothing much wrong with them. As for the rest, there were too many to mention. Some were particularly notable.

One old lady came with an enormous dermoid growth about half the size of her head on the back of her skull and eating its way into her cranial cavity. There was also a poor little girl who had a complex corneal injury with desperate ulceration and an unusable eye which was scheduled for evisceration. There were lots of people with huge spleens. Such a clinical finding would likely be a teaching case in the UK but just about

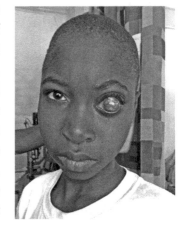

every local patient sported massive splenic enlargement. This results from a condition called portal hypertension, in turn the result of a chronic infection called schistosomiasis (sometimes called bilharzia) that is picked up from the local river water. Almost all the local people are exposed to river water on a daily basis so bilharzia is endemic. There were others too. Patients with glaucoma, abdominal swelling, curious ultrasound abnormalities, a couple of sick looking young girls, one with aplastic anaemia and one who probably had recurrent pulmonary TB. Some were told to come back for tests, for glasses, for a check. Some were told to go home: "There's nothing wrong with you." Not many seemed overjoyed to hear that.

It was lovely to finally spend some time with and share dinner with David and Lorraine McAdam. Some of the missionary lads announced that they were going out on the river on a "croc hunt." To me this seemed seriously mad. In total darkness, nursing a big gun on a tiny open boat on a dangerous river – not my idea of an evening's entertainment! The plan was to take a

David and Lorraine McAdam

powerful searchlight and scan around for the monster crocodile responsible for taking the life of a little boy the previous week. In fact, there had been several attacks over the past month or so. As we sat drinking coffee, we heard a couple of shots go off. One small croc killed. The big guy escaped on this occasion.

29

I returned to my house and was sorting out some stuff when a quad bike rolled up outside. It was pitch black - you could almost feel the darkness. No starlight or moonlight. David had been called to the delivery room for a 17 year old girl failing to progress in her labour. Oxytocin had been given and a vacuum delivery attempted without success. So we took her to theatre for Caesarian section. There was much meconium staining around the baby who was pretty flat and flaccid following delivery. Thankfully, after a while and following some active resuscitation, the baby started to breathe.

We planned to meet at the hospital the following morning to see the inpatients and then to perform surgery on a particularly tragic case. The plan was to carry out a gastrostomy (the placing of a semi-permanent feeding tube through the abdominal wall into the stomach) in a young man who had an oesophageal stricture resulting from the ingestion of battery acid a couple of months before. It appears that some people when hurt or offended will attempt to make the perpetrator of their misery feel bad by self-harming. A popular method appears to be the ingestion of this caustic poison; presumably they do this while completely unaware of the devastating consequences.

Orientation

September and October in Zambia is about the hottest time of year. All the vegetation looks like it has been burned to a crisp. When I arrived in the hospital, I was impressed by the collection of really awful clinical problems. As I wandered the wards with David, there seemed to be a succession of insoluble problems. The variety and severity of these cases was dizzying. There were patients with tuberculosis, myeloma, advanced metastatic cancer of unknown origin, two ladies with recurrent cervical cancer, another with a crocodile attack injury to her lower leg, a young man with a fractured cervical spine and paraplegia. The list went on and on - a patient with a swollen tender leg and a solid lower abdominal mass, another with a snake bite, not to mention patients with various fractures, medical conditions such as glaucoma, hypertension and rheumatic heart disease and a whole host of people with a collection of symptoms which remained undiagnosed.

We took the chap with the caustic oesophageal stricture to theatre to take a look at the damage with a flexible endoscope and prepare for his gastrostomy. The scope only passed to 25 cm from the front teeth at which point the lumen narrowed to a pin point opening. I doubted that this could be fixed short of oesophagectomy (surgical removal of the gullet) and replacement with a loop of colon. That would be a massive undertaking here! We carried out an abdominal operation to place the tube but found the stomach to be horribly contracted, thick walled and scarred and very difficult to bring to a high midline abdominal incision. Clearly the battery acid had produced more damage than anticipated. It seemed obvious that a gastrostomy would not serve him well for feeding. Instead we had to perform a jejunostomy which involves using a loop of intestine further downstream from the stomach to allow a tube to be tunneled into place and secured. We can only hope that this will allow him to have some nourishment and gain strength while we figure out whether a more definitive major procedure might be possible.

After lunch, I was given a quick tutorial on the basic controls of a quad bike then Chris sped off to give me a tour of the whole area. I almost turned the machine over on one heavily rutted track but recovered with the help of a couple of local lads. We visited the colony, an area that had been housing for leprosy patients and the Old Hospital where patients basically hang about until they can be seen or operated on. There they live in little booths or rooms, sit around outside whiling away the time and cook their meals on an open fire in the courtyard. We drove along to some of the nearby villages. Essentially these were collections of mud brick houses with grass roofs. There were young children everywhere, all happy to call out to me and pose for photos. We visited Chambula Chimwanga, a committed local Christian and teacher in the government school. I recognised the distinctive Manchester United shirt he wore as an avid supporter and he was keen to keep me informed of the half time score at Old Trafford! It was not good news and he was most concerned at the poor performance! His two sons rejoice in the names of Marvellous and Prince Philip. Prince Philip turned out to be an extremely mischievous character!

We went down by the river where, in the expansive flood plain, there were several groups of men building or working in the kilns used to harden mud bricks.

Another eventful day and the definite need for a cold shower to reset my thermostat!

Disappointment
The following day turned out to have a really pathetic quality - I'll come to the reason shortly.

I was wandering along towards the house after a Sunday church service with Emma, a Canadian nurse, and the amazing Dr Mwansa (a local Zambian doctor) when David came along on the quad bike and said there was a problem with the tiny baby born by section late on Friday night. She had been reasonably well if a bit anaemic on her first day. The blood sugar levels kept dropping and to be honest I am not sure that the nurses were really switched on to doing anything much about that. When we arrived, the baby appeared moribund. I was pretty sure she was already dead but we did manage to get her oxygen saturation up from about 55% to around 70% at best. Without ventilation, however, it just dropped away. She had a fluid challenge and some more dextrose but arrested very soon afterwards. What a great shame. The whole perinatal care was essentially educated guesswork with no laboratory data to guide and direct each move. I suspect she would have survived in a neonatal ICU. Out here? A downward clinical spiral is a truly ominous sign.

I was expecting a quiet afternoon. Listened to a podcast and did some reading but there was more clinical action to shatter the peace. One call was for a strange young man who presented somewhat uncommunicative and confused, but without focal neurological signs. He had been agitated but by the time we saw him had settled down a lot. There was no obvious upset in vital signs although had he had a fever, I suppose a cerebral abscess would have been well up the list of possibilities. One for observation and masterly inactivity!

Then, after attempting to cool down (unsuccessfully), there was another call. A woman in labour had gone a bit mad. She was in the final stages of her delivery but was walking around and refusing to push. ("Too sore" - I can well believe that!) David gave her a spinal anaesthetic and when we had her lie down on the operating table it looked like the baby was virtually there. I put the Ventouse vacuum extractor on and she delivered with minimal help. My major triumph was managing not to drop the baby. Babies are extremely slippery customers! This one needed a fair bit of encouragement to breathe but seemed in good shape. When we left, I was wondering how many more completely new things I could cope with at this rate.

Groinery: A specialty in its own right

In the early morning, a stroll to the hospital presents the most comfortable temperature of the day. Outside it was nice and cool, a complete change to the relentless heat of the day that is both fierce and energy sapping.

I reviewed a couple of patients who had been listed for surgery. One almost certainly had a small fluid swelling (hydrocoele) resulting from a septic condition. The scarring that had been left would have made surgery difficult. The lesion was small and not very symptomatic so in this elderly man (he claimed to be 94 but I had my doubts!) I felt we should leave him well alone. The other patient could possibly have been left also. We scanned him to confirm another hydrocoele, again almost certainly due to prior infection. He was in more discomfort and since he came from 270 km away we took the opportunity of doing a quick operation on him. It served the double benefit of helping the patient and teaching Mwansa how to do this particular procedure. See one, do one, teach one!

Our operating list for the morning was:

- Total abdominal hysterectomy with unilateral salpingoophorectomy in a 43 year old woman with a huge fibroid uterus causing anaemia.

- Bilateral tubal ligation in a young woman who was 3 days postpartum.

- A hydrocoele in an old boy of 80 under local and with a touch of ketamine.

- Umbilical hernia repair in a young lad who presented acutely over the weekend.

After the hydrocoele, I suddenly felt sweaty and light-headed so sat down beside the air conditioner and felt better after a glass of water. What a horrible sensation. I was glad we had no other customers fasted for surgery that day.

At 12:55 I headed off with Emma, Christina, another Canadian nurse, and Chris for lunch with Dorothy Woodside, a senior missionary originally from California. She lives alone in a substantial house. For many years she was the only ex-pat medical worker on the mission station here. Now there are a large number of chronic patients for whom she takes responsibility. The house appeared to be full of chaotic clutter. It was dark, inside and out. Dorothy is fearless! And hospitable! The house was amazing; full of boxes of supplies, Bibles and literature not to mention bags of vegetables, maize, kasava and all manner of other crops. Boxes of all shapes and sizes required a little care to navigate. The furniture had stood the test of time and there were numerous books and pictures (many of Yosemite) with evidence of busy-ness all around. Industry, with just a delightful sprinkling of eccentricity!

I wandered back to my house in the afternoon. Thankfully there was no more hospital action which is just as well because I had no energy, felt hot and slightly nauseated. Maybe the sausages, mustard, sauerkraut, carrots and papaya were to blame.

Lurking danger

By the following morning I was raring to go. Thankfully there have been no post-operative problems so far! Amazing! The nursing staff does not inspire confidence. They are nice enough, a bit laid back (actually extremely laid back). They generally speak good English but can be a little less than diligent in matters of routine care. Despite the best efforts, the wards are not clean. It would be virtually impossible to keep them clean. They also need a better system for processing rubbish and instruments from theatre. It is all the more remarkable that there are not more post-operative complications.

Almost all of the patients for today were operated under spinal anaesthesia. These cases were for hernias, benign prostatic enlargement and sundry gynaecological conditions. Without a professional anaesthetist we have to do our own spinal anaesthetics. I surprised myself by achieving good block within a minute or two. As I cast my mind back to practice in Glasgow, it did make me wonder what on earth our anaesthetists get up to. They can fankle about and can make a spinal last for 20 minutes without difficulty. Maybe these cases were just easy. I am sure my anaesthetic colleagues have a similar high regard for surgical speed or the lack thereof!

I hadn't done an open prostate operation for years – since I was a junior trainee in the Western Infirmary in Glasgow in 1982 in fact. It felt rather like riding a bike in that each component of the operation just seemed to fall into place and the patient parted with a nice big juicy 75g prostate.

After another spinal for a prostate cancer case, we carried out the evisceration of the blind eye in the wee 12 year old girl. Her dad was desperately keen that we give her an artificial eye. Unfortunately, there are none here! He was told she could possibly get one later. I felt very sorry for them. The girl was very stoical about the whole thing.

I wandered down to the river after theatre and met several local folk carrying wood or water and usually with babies strapped to their backs. Had a chat with a local man arriving to bathe. The topic - crocodiles. He was unfazed as he headed towards the river and I headed up the hill! I hope he survived.

Mental

I woke to the depressing news about the migrant issues in the Mediterranean and about deceptive ISIS fighters finding their way into European cities and flying their flags, ideologies and techniques while the governments appear to drift with no sign of much of a response. These issues hold no interest for the people here who struggle for survival day and daily.

As I spent time in the wards, I developed a clearer idea of the spectrum of disease. For a Western doctor it is almost unbelievable. First, I was speechless to learn that despite my prostatectomy patient being in 'intensive care' and despite me visiting him at 9pm last night in case he was bleeding and in spite of me asking the nursing staff to make sure he was given adequate pain control and an IV fluid challenge because he was clammy, sore and his circulation seemed peripherally shut down, when I saw him, not a single observation of vital signs had been made overnight! He basically lay there all night and no one even bothered to check on him. There is one very experienced senior nurse here called Julie Rachel Elwood. She's from

Northern Ireland, works tirelessly and provides the midwifery as well as being the anaesthetist, endoscopist and, sometimes, the surgical registrar! She (politely) went ballistic at the staff. Amazingly enough, the patient was unharmed; more because of his robust physiology than the post-operative care! I was invited to be responsible for teaching the clinical team next week. The topic was an easy choice. *'Patient safety and essential post-operative monitoring.'*

The rest of the ward round was an amazing collection of the local morbidity. There was a road accident victim shipped in by ambulance from Zambezi and two patients recovering from crocodile attacks. One girl had the presence of mind to turn the beast over as it had a hold of her lower leg. She managed to actually sit on it and scream for help. She did require some fancy plastic surgery and skin grafting but was recovering well. The rest of the round was a blur of chest infections, profound anaemias, all sorts of sepsis including the classical STDs; gonococcal arthritis, syphilis, HIV, even rheumatic heart disease (which is virtually gone from the UK and I can just about remember as a student in Scotland); it's very common here. Mercifully, the walking wounded from yesterday's operating list were all fine.

One crucial component of the day in Chitokoloki Mission Hospital is tea-break. It is sacrosanct and must not be violated. Even although the queue for the clinic almost reached from the door to the operating department all the way to the front door of the building - I would guesstimate about 90-100 patients; the tea break continued unabated. It provides a chance to draw breath, swap stories, discuss the filling of the swimming pool (today), arrange social activities and brace ourselves for the onslaught. Lunch is also sacrosanct and always served at 1pm sharp.

I spent the day working my way through dozens of cases with the help of an interpreter, examining most, scanning some with a portable ultrasound machine, booking operations which sounds grander than the reality which is basically telling the patients to pitch up the following day, fasted and then they wait to see if there is any possibility of an operation. If not, they keep coming back until they finally get their treatment. Most of the patients presenting like this in the UK would be sent to the appropriate specialist. Most would have several investigations. Those with vague symptoms or obvious signs of serious pathology would get a CT scan or an MRI. Here, it is educated guesswork. I suppose it is a bit like veterinary practice. Case histories are scanty and somewhat unreliable. Communication is difficult

and requires interpretation. Patients seem to have a tendency to tell you what they think you want to hear.

Some of us went to a Bible study session in the evening. I came out into the pitch black night with only my phone for a torch. Was chatting to a couple of the Canadians when there was a lot of shouting and excitement very close by. I was not able to figure out quite what was happening till I managed to get my phone light on. Here was a very excited ox kicking and jumping about only 3-4 yards away. Its handlers were yelling and had absolutely no control. As we scarpered, I instantly thought of the chap in the hospital who needs reconstructive abdominal surgery following a bad goring. It is so dark that you really cannot see your hand in front of you and when danger lurks and strange noises emerge it is rather unsettling.

Chris the pilot and Joey the engineer went croc hunting again last night. This time they saw the beast but couldn't get a shot away. The locals are still really scared. It will be a good day when they get a bullet in its head. Now that it has experience of preying on people the stakes seem to rise and the belief is that more will now be at risk.

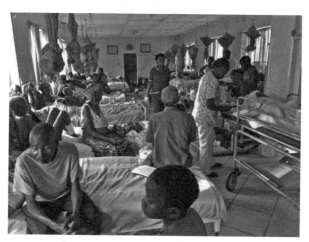

The male ward including floor beds

Koomadiki

People have often asked me about the difficulties of providing a Western style clinical service in the African bush. In reality, with some experience, a sprinkling of confidence and a good internet connection one can accomplish a great deal more than you might imagine. When the connection drops, it can be an added trial. I had been attempting to keep up with the BBC News but the signal kept dropping out. I did manage to get one brief travel report about the traffic on the M25. Fat lot of good that information is to me here! However, today I had cause to reflect on waiting times. Patients here come along, get their blue 'ticket' which passes for a case record and if a decision is made for further examination, X-ray, ultrasound or operation they hear a Lunda word which I have come to recognise. 'Koomadiki' - i.e. come 'tomorrow.' And often when they come tomorrow, there is a fair chance that they may hear the same message until finally their time comes. We have not been in the habit of making up an operating list as such. The koomadiki patients from yesterday queue up at the operating theatre department and sit with their tickets until they are called in.

It is evident that a clear gradation in the value and importance of medical treatment exists. Pills are not very highly regarded and even really important medicine like the life-preserving antiretroviral therapy for HIV patients often doesn't get taken. I saw a chap with HIV, cytomegalovirus infection with oesophagitis, unable to eat and in considerable pain. Considering the options, which are not plentiful, we decided to check that he was taking his medicine. Sadly, the very thing that had a chance to help him was being avoided. So, pills are not high on the pecking order. Injections; these are an altogether more prestigious treatment modality. However, surgery is the pinnacle. If you need an operation, that is top line treatment! Irrespective of the indication or the likely benefit - surgery is what is required! However, it will be koomadiki at the earliest!

Today a flight from Chingola arrived halfway through the operating list. On board were two patients; one from South Africa for a minor procedure and the other from Beith in Ayrshire - for some endoscopic work. The Scot is a teacher on the mission station there and has been in Africa for 25 years or so. We then went back to running two theatres, David doing the cataracts while I took care of the various cases in the queue. Anaesthesia is interesting here. General anaesthesia is really only used for major abdominal cases and for some tiny babies. Local anaesthetic is the best option for hernias and the run of the mill 'groinery,' and spinals with or without an injection of ketamine for most lower abdominal work. It is a truly amazing drug, unbelievably useful. Who needs anaesthetists? I am now more convinced than ever that for the vast majority of work (at least here) you can stick in a spinal and by the time you have scrubbed (using river water which is possibly alive with schistosomiasis), gowned and gloved, the patient is ready for 'knife to skin.'

Just as I was leaving for the day, I got a call from the emergency room. A lad presented from Zambezi following a road accident with what appears to be early intestinal obstruction. I think a conservative approach appeals. There is always koomadiki!

Sorry to say Dr. Mwansa Jere is heading off for a holiday tomorrow. Mwansa is an extraordinarily gifted doctor. She was raised in Lusaka and after high school there spent a gap year in China and learned Chinese. She then decided to stay longer and went to medical school, in China and was taught in Chinese! When she returned to Zambia the Ministry of Health posted her to Chitokoloki which was a wonderful fit because she is also a keen Christian. It is a shame she is leaving us because she is a fantastic help, a gifted surgeon and full of local knowledge. Emma Wichers, one of the Canadian nurses, is also flying out tomorrow. She is off to be married and will certainly be missed.

I have yet to meet my house worker. She comes when I am in the hospital. When I came back to the house to make my lunch today (the first day I have not been a guest elsewhere for a sumptuous and delicious lunch), I was exploring the well-stocked larder, considering whether pasta with chicken or tuna or meat sauce, planning to collect my selection and head for the pot cupboard. I happened to open the fridge and there was a joyous sight. Some kind soul had already prepared my lunch for me. Right on the plate, roast chicken, green beans, corn, potatoes and barbecue sauce. Talk about service!

Lessons learned and mysterious Mary.

Most of the time we learn stuff on the fly or as a result of experience, also known as trial and error. Sometimes though, it is really important to pay close attention to certain details. Failing to learn such lessons can result in misery. Here are some of the important lessons I have learned this week and one that I have taught.

*Learned lesson #1.*Keep your mouth closed in the shower. It's no big deal at home of course, but when your water supply comes from the Zambezi river the last thing you want to ingest is the bug that results in the majority of the local population having chronic disease, portal hypertension and a huge liver and spleen. I am happy with my spleen the way it is!

Learned lesson #2. Never run the tap when cleaning your teeth. I almost caught myself falling into this trap. The reason is the same. Contaminated water! Even if more and more of the water is coming from a bore-hole I still dread to think what parasites might reside therein. Apart from the schistosomes you could choose from hookworm, roundworm, tapeworm, amoebic dysentery, bacillary dysentery not to mention typhoid and any number of viral illnesses that could come by that route. Using filtered water from the fridge for dental hygiene is all well and good although it is a bit of a fiddle. However, the temptation to stick your toothbrush under the running tap is hard to resist. It is a virtually automatic, almost reflex action. Note to self. Never run the tap when cleaning teeth!

Learned lesson #3. Always carefully tuck the mosquito net in all around the bed every time you enter. Again a bit of a nuisance but who wants to be bitten mercilessly by some crack team of mosquitoes on the rampage for a blood meal. I saw two nasty looking insects up close today. As it happens both had flown into patients' ears and got stuck. Two different patients. Same problem. So far no bites I have been aware of and so far only a few crickets or similar but no real nasties although there was a cockroach in the scrub sink in theatre the other day.

Taught lesson #1. A lesson in shaving. I had to intervene when I saw Kayumbo trying to dry shave the sensitive parts of a lower abdomen in preparation for surgery. He was using a hand held plastic razor. Simple, right? Wrong! This might seem ridiculous but there is a way NOT to perform this little operation and that was exactly the technique being used. My authority on the topic comes partly from empirical observation and from personal experience of using a razor every morning! I am conscious that telling this story might not only revolutionise the clearing of hair from abdomens in Chitokoloki but could potentially transform analogous procedures for faces and other anatomical areas amongst the less initiated. Patience! The crucial tip is coming up!

Almost every one who attempts to use a razor, in my view, uses it incorrectly and inefficiently. The usual modus operandi is to make a cutting stroke, lift the blade, reposition, make another cutting stroke and so on. After the first cutting stroke the blade fouls up with hair and the successive strokes are progressively less effective.

Then you need to manually clear the blade, which can easily result in injury if you use your finger and move in the wrong direction. The correct method is to make sure that the blade maintains contact with the skin continually. Do not lift it off at all. Cutting strokes and back-strokes can then quickly and easily achieve the desired effect, each back stroke clears the trapped hair and when you learn this lesson it revolutionises your approach to hirsute issues. Kayumbo's face lit up when he tried it. He shaved several more patients that day smiling and laughing at how easy it was. So at least I'll be remembered for something here!

Today was another long day in the clinic. First though, we all assembled at the airstrip at 7:15 to see Emma and Mwansa off the premises. The day finished with another gathering at the airstrip just before sunset to welcome some more visitors. Kevin Kerrigan, a surgeon from Spokane, Washington and his wife, Lesley and a junior doctor from England. I could see that we'd have both theatres running the next week!

Lunch was with a Canadian family (Shawn and Rhonda Markle) one of whose two girls (Mackenzie) was having her tenth birthday. It was a lovely lunch preceded by an Oreo game (start with the Oreo on your forehead and get it into you mouth without using hands but by using various facial gestures!) Then the girls provided a 'show,' a performance featuring dancing, hula hoops and three songs from 'The Lion King'. The performance lasted 9 minutes 19 seconds according to the programme. David McAdam managed to sleep for a good few of the minutes but since he was behind an insect screen no one noticed!

In between times, a heavy clinic; patients with chest infections, TB, eye problems, hypertension, pelvic inflammatory disease and, of course, various cancers. Two patients stood out for me. Both were young women and both with very treatable conditions but both of whom have no hope of survival out here. One had cervical cancer. A nasty, locally advanced tumour and in the first world she would almost certainly have her life saved by radiation with chemotherapy and possibly surgery. Here, there is no prospect of meaningful treatment. Even if she were in Lusaka, it is doubtful that she would be able to access the care she needs. The other is a young woman with a leaking heart valve resulting from rheumatic fever years before. She needs that valve replaced, almost a routine procedure in Scotland. Here, she will probably be dead in a matter of months from advancing cardiac failure. Tragic.

On the way back tonight, I wandered into the Old Hospital with my camera to find people drawing water from a bore hole. They live in little compartments built into the wall. It is desperate. Dozens of children came after me to be photographed or to grab my hand and stroke my arm and giggle when I showed them the pictures I took of them. At least two tiny kids who were in their mother's arms took one look at me as I walked by and screamed blue murder. I didn't appreciate that I could be so frightening.

As for Mary? She apparently is my house worker and although I had been here for more than a week we had not met. It seems that she is the one responsible for the phantom lunch yesterday and the nicely folded laundry a few days ago. She has also left some kind of savoury chicken bake for my dinner tonight. Chris the pilot, who is next door, had the same dish left in his fridge and he came in to use the microwave in the house I have been given. Mary is a top girl! I am looking forward to meeting her.

Sans eyes, sans teeth

I made my first real foray into dentistry today. David showed me the techniques for dental local anaesthesia for both upper and lower jaws. I removed a rotten upper 1st premolar using a device called a root elevator. Fang farrier extraordinaire! It's amazing what you can do with a modified screwdriver!

I have also tried to get my bearings with a logical approach to eye problems. There are lots of eye infections as well as cataracts, uveitis and glaucoma. Using a combination of visual acuity

testing, pupil dilatation, fundoscopy and intraocular pressure measurement, we can have a pretty good stab at a diagnosis. For some things, not much can be done. However, we treated a young woman yesterday in acute distress with severe conjunctivitis and pus pouring from both eyes. A wee touch of tetracycline eye ointment and gentamicin drops and she was smiling and happy and totally transformed by this morning. One very happy customer.

When David can't find much wrong with someone's eyes, he generally says: 'Try her with a pair of glasses', whereupon a drawer is pulled open and a selection is made from a large number of antiquated reading glasses. We make a best guess at the strength +1, +2 etc. and the patient is chased out the door! Bemused!

Last week's post-operative major cases are doing well. The hysterectomy patient has been sent home. The elderly man following open prostatectomy is not quite ready but slowly improving. The acid swallower in whom I attempted and failed with a feeding gastrostomy insertion is now tolerating liquid food through his jejunostomy tube.

I was also introduced to the joys of protein refractometry to assess the protein content of peritoneal fluid. In the UK, a sample is sent to the lab and you can expect the result the following day. Here, we can use a very cool device and get an instant result. It allows a handy distinction to be made for a patient with a fluid filled abdomen between a transudate (from something like cirrhosis) and an exudate (which might herald a tumour or abdominal TB).

After work, I tried to sit outside in the sun for a while. Gave up after 15 minutes. Far too hot.

Having decided to go for a wander to stretch my legs about 4:30pm I saw Kaitlin, one of the nurses, racing towards the hospital on her quad bike. I couldn't resist the temptation to go and poke my nose in. Good grief. Talk about dentistry. Here I witnessed the extremes of dental conditions in one day! The premolar that bit the dust was one end of the spectrum. This patient in the emergency room was close to death from, of all things, a dental abscess! This was a young man as systemically septic a patient as I have seen for a long time. His pulse was racing at 160/min and he was short of breath. His dental abscess must have started 2 or 3 weeks before in Angola and he had been to the witch doctor. He had a kind of branding mark over his left upper chest wall. The abscess had eaten away the tissues below his chin and the infection then spread around his neck and down over his chest eroding the skin on the front of his neck and leaving a large defect over his right upper chest about 10-12cm in diameter. The main portion of his pectoralis major muscle was clearly visible as was his thyroid and trachea. I would never have believed such a thing was possible. Anyway, I took him to theatre and with a slug of ketamine cleared all the infected and dead tissue. Whether he would survive the night, I had no idea. He certainly had a chest X-ray that would fit with the ARDS Acute Respiratory Distress Syndrome - a critical problem that often accompanies severe infection. Time will tell. I can almost guarantee that no dentist has ever seen or dealt with such a case in the developed world.

J-R Construction

Haven't seen a cloud for 10 days. Having cloud withdrawal.

I was able to give some teaching in the church and my talk was translated into Lunda by Chambula (he has the two sons, Marvellous and Prince Philip!). The audience was very appreciative and delighted to receive greetings from Christians in Scotland.

I wandered, very late, to the hospital to see the damage from last night. Happily, the chap who was close to death has improved a good deal. I decided to take him back to theatre to change his dressings and cleared a load of blood clot from under the skin flaps and the abscess cavity. Ketamine is marvellous stuff - you can get away with doing virtually anything to a patient, it just seems to switch the brain off altogether.

Julie Rachel Elwood (J-R) is one of the experienced and wonderfully talented nurses here who does a bit of everything. She gives anaesthetics, delivers babies and provides on call cover for the hospital. She treats all sorts of emergencies, can provide an elective service for babies with club foot even performing judicious surgical division of the Achilles tendon where necessary. Beyond the clinical work she transports the old, the blind and infirm to church in a trailer pulled along by her quad bike and she runs classes of various kinds and she builds houses!

Remarkable! She was collecting grass for a thatch; a job for an old couple who live out in the villages and who have no one to look out for them. Their old house was dilapidated and not suitable for habitation. J-R built them a new house. Mud bricks and a thatched roof. She had to hide and store the grass off site because the other locals likely would have stolen it. So the house is now complete. Not a stick of furniture but at least the old couple have a chance of staying protected when the rains come in the next few weeks. By all accounts the rain here can be very heavy. There are no surfaced roads around - just a lot of sand and simple tracks. It will be a real mess when the heavy rain arrives.

Tribalism is alive and well in Africa. The hierarchy is a little difficult to figure out. There are various identities with varying responsibilities and reporting duties including the head man, the chief and the system of local councillors. There are also the healers, witch doctors, herbalists, quasi-Christian witch doctors and even osteopath-type bone setters. Of course, they have no training and no clear idea what they are doing and often end up creating a lot of damage. It seems that people go to the hospital as a last resort. Just like our man last night who almost lost his life to overwhelming infection.

It turns out David is a rich source of politically incorrect quotable quotes and aphorisms. Here is a selection from lunchtime today:

- 'Nurses should not go to university. Nonsense!'
- 'They teach all sorts of ridiculous things at universities these days! There should only be three courses at a university. Medicine, Law, and Engineering!' 'What about chemistry David?' 'That's engineering.'
- 'We had an American gynaecologist here who couldn't put in a canula or do a spinal. When he managed a canula there was whooping and cheering in theatre. When he managed a spinal he did a kind of dance. Totally useless! We were better off with our medical students and some of them hadn't done much.'

Chavuma

Chavuma is a town at the back of beyond. It has a hospital that sits on a hill near the Zambezi River and close to the Angolan border. There are four wards, an operating theatre and an outpatients building. The wards surround a courtyard with an enormous mango tree laden with (unripe) fruit. The flight to Chavuma from Chitokoloki took about 35 minutes. Smooth flying but thick haze

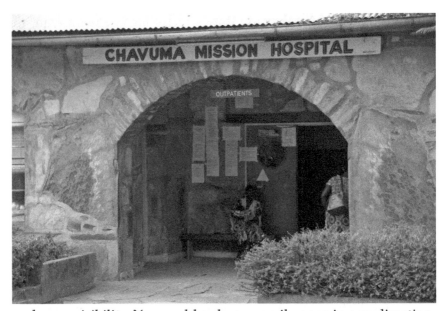

and poor visibility. You could only see a mile or so in any direction. There were four of us on board. David McAdam, myself, Kayumbo and Chris the pilot. He offered me the chance to take off from Chitokoloki. I did have an active pilots licence some years ago but have not done much flying for a few years. Actually the plane, a Cessna 210, virtually flies itself. You get to an airspeed of about 52 knots, lift the nose and you're airborne. Coming in to Chavuma was a bit rough. The approach was fine but the airstrip is rough and bumpy. We then had to drive in a rickety old Land Cruiser for about 15 minutes on deeply rutted sandy tracks through scrub and bush until we finally reached the town. It has a school, a massive anthill, a few shops including a butcher. The butcher's dog was outside what passed for the shop and what a miserable scrawny looking specimen he was! Doesn't say much for the quality of the meat. There were lots of curious locals around to welcome us. There are two Christian Japanese nurses in Chavuma and they basically run the hospital. They provide a fantastic service to the local community. Again, we encountered a collection of weird and wonderful tumours and swellings. Again, lots of eye disease. Several people blinded because

the witch doctors poured boiling water in their eyes to get rid of their problem. Unbelievable! Yet it has happened to lots of people.

David went off to do a clinic and I operated on 8 cases. Minor stuff, mostly under ketamine or local. The list was punctuated by a full lunch at the home of one of the local missionaries. We flew back into Chitokoloki as the sun was setting. Tried to make a video as we turned finals to land. After a long but very interesting day I was ready to put my feet up for a while and read.

A day of gastric and colorectal cases had been set up for following day so time to break out the surgical staplers I brought from Scotland in the hope we have enough people to run two operating rooms. There is a never-ending supply of patients requiring major surgery such that it just feels like an avalanche that keeps going.

Controlled violence

Some days at Chitokoloki are particularly

demanding. As the team grappled all day with a succession of operations, lurking concern continued for the progress of Angolan Moses (Mr. Dental Abscess). He seemed to be hanging in and holding his own while he fights on against the threatening sepsis. It was unfortunate that he lost more and more skin as each day passed. I went to deal with his dressings towards the end of the day only to find maggots crawling through the dressings and all over the wound. There are few scenarios more likely to make you gag. The sight and smell in combination was hard to describe – just putrid. Really gross! I decided to leave the maggots in place on the basis that they are probably the best way to deal with dead tissue. You can actually get medical maggots for wound care at home although they cost a fortune and come packaged in a little teabag like pouch. These African maggots were the free-range wild-type! Kevin Kerrigan, the American surgeon, also ran an operating list so between us we motored through such a load of cases that we reached the point where there were no beds available for any more. The bed occupancy statistics in Chitokoloki would translate poorly into the NHS. While real beds are required for post-operative cases, regular patients can always have a bed. If there is no conventional bed space, mattresses are placed on the floor so you can multiply the number of inpatients quite readily. If the mattresses run out, I reckon patients would readily sleep on the floor, under other beds or wherever. Fortunately the pressure on space failed to reach such critical levels but I can well imagine that it might. It is good to have an occasional clear out of the 'walking wounded' by which means it is usually possible to create the necessary space.

We had the pleasure today of having the assistance of Dr Joel Nkonde from Loloma. Joel is a single-handed Congolese doctor who is based at Loloma Mission Hospital. Loloma is some 155km east of Chitokoloki and while Joel has had some surgical training he understandably hesitates to take on very major or ambitious cases on his own, especially when his support is even less than that available at Chitokoloki. I can think of several occasions when Joel has literally driven his patients from Loloma to Chitokoloki in his own car – bumping them along over un-surfaced roads for most of the way. He had never used the surgical stapling guns before so it was fun to let him loose with a little gentle guidance. As we left the hospital at 6pm, a little 4 year old boy was brought in. His mum had walked for two hours to carry him to hospital. He had a penetrating eye injury from a sharp stick or a thorn. David took him to theatre and dealt with his corneal tear and prolapsing iris. Hopefully he should do well.

Pool volleyball

Some days are designated for outpatient work. These can be just as tiring and demanding as operating days. A common problem for me relates to the real difficulty I have in making sense of most of the records. The system is unique and customised for this site only. It is very different from what might be described as a 'proper' medical records system. Each patient is given a blue card. This is their 'ticket' and essentially comprises their entire medical record. I could imagine that such a system might have utility however, its success would be dependent on two qualities – completeness and legibility. Unfortunately, the system frequently fails on both counts. Most of the staff working in Chitokoloki have now completely given up trying to read David McAdam's hieroglyphics – his writing is so illegible that the best one can do is try to make an educated guess at the message he has put on the record.

I eventually baled out and made better use of my time in theatre. An additional advantage is that in theatre you can be physically closer to the only working air conditioner in the hospital. It was a good excuse, therefore, to get on with some endoscopic work while others continued to see the clinic customers. It was not unusual to struggle home at the end of the day feeling drained and lacking in energy. The heat at this time of year seems to sap your strength. I am so impressed that the permanent staff have the stamina to keep going. I only hope that the patients, who are seen promptly, efficiently and for no charge, appreciate the commitment shown by the missionaries who run this place.

Today provided an opportunity to respond to a standing invitation to make my way to the pool. This is an almost instant way to feel better, to switch off, relax, cool down and occasionally be drawn into a game of pool volleyball. The rules are flexibly interpreted such that Dr McAdam's team is placed at an advantage on any dubious line calls or other infringements. This was the situation irrespective of either the justice of any claim or the score, unless the McAdam team was in a comfortable lead.

Operating

Living in the African bush cocoons you off from the rest of the world. The geo-political tensions that occupy the Western world just simply seem irrelevant here. I found that one feature of getting up at 6:45am here is that one can tune in to BBC Radio 4 on the internet and hear 'Tweet of the Day' every day. I got to hoping that they might soon run out of birds. It has to be one of the least functional time fillers on the media. The international news is of little consequence to Chitokoloki – no one has any real reason to care about the arguments over which our politicians work themselves into a lather.

Amongst the theatre cases for the day there was a call concerning a crocodile attack. The story just did not add up. A little girl was brought to the hospital after she had apparently been bathing in the river and she came out of the water with blood around her midriff. The clinical team was instantly suspicious. She was taken for a careful examination under anaesthetic and the conclusion was that she had probably been the victim of a sexual assault. No two days are the same – even surgically. In Scotland, theatre lists take on a familiar pattern. Not here – every specialty can feature and it would not be unusual to follow a Caesarian section case with someone who needed a below knee amputation for a gangrenous diabetic foot. Adaptability is a useful quality.

"Throw your bones on the bed"

One curious thing about the local people is that they have no concept about how to climb into a bed or onto an examination couch. We don't think about this in the West but they typically don't have beds at home and if you ask someone to climb onto a trolley they get confused and either end up with their legs in some strange position or their head finds its way to the wrong end of the bed and their feet finish on the pillow. Actually pillows hardly exist here. No one uses pillows in the bush. Grass mats are probably more straightforward. Following operation the patients are lifted into a bed without a pillow and to my eye they looked really uncomfortable. Despite that, I have never heard a complaint.

While regular clinic days can be chaotic, the confusion and chaos can multiply almost beyond recognition when the visiting orthopaedic team makes one of their regular scheduled two day visits. They fly in under the banner of Flyspec[6] a medical charity set up in 1982 by Professor John Jellis who was a senior orthopaedic surgeon at the University Teaching Hospital in Lusaka. Flyspec operate two Cessna aircraft and both orthopaedic and plastic surgery teams come to Chitokoloki on a regular basis to help patients who need such specialised input. The orthopaedic group will sometimes bring two surgeons or one surgeon and an orthotist, but they always see a vast crowd of patients and advise on their ongoing care. Some are directed for procedures of some sort, plaster changes or they may be listed for surgery the following day.

A fairly common problem here is the occurence of long bone fractures in young patients. The young adults usually sustain them by falling off a motorbike or an ox cart. The children, of whom there are many, fall out of trees. Some of the mangoes are beginning to ripen so they scramble up the trees and not infrequently fall out sustaining a 'mango fracture.' They end up in bed for weeks on end with their leg in traction, sometimes with a Steinmann pin through their tibia. This is a high price to pay for a hard mango but it is good to have some specialist bone doctors to supervise their recovery.

In the wards - mild confusion continually reigns. There are ultrasound examinations galore - it's the only instant imaging modality available and a great deal of educated guesswork provides a means of making progress. Unfortunately, the patients are not monitored adequately and given that we have no laboratory values, for many it is difficult to form a clear idea of what might be going on. Diagnosis and treatment advances as a series of marginally informed conjecture with little chance of proving anything. Amazingly enough, all our major surgical and orthopaedic cases seem to have avoided any significant complications. This hospital has no showers and no baths. Bathing patients basically means a kind of a bed bath. Some of the patients would benefit from being taken out and hosed down. Beyond that, I never cease to be astonished at the resilience of the local Zambian patients. Many of them are chronically anaemic. This can be produced by malaria, bilharzia and any number of other causes that are not specific to rural Africa. Both malaria and bilharzia are particularly common here – maybe more common than just about anywhere else on the planet! It is little wonder that some seem to be lethargic and it is beyond me that people can even function with such profound anaemia that it hardly seems compatible with life. Some present with haemoglobin levels down at 3 grams per deciliter (g/dL). Haemoglobin is the oxygen transporting protein in red blood cells and when the level is low, tissues are starved of life giving oxygen and the result can vary from heart attacks, strokes, severe breathlessness, kidney disease and an inability to exercise or move around without feeling utterly exhausted. The normal range for men is 13.5 to 17.5g/dL and for women, 12.0 to 15.5 g/dL. The lowest I saw on presentation in Chitokoloki so far was a level of 1.7g/dL!

Friday is a clinic day with the typical range of every complaint known to man. I was always impressed with the variety and having to come up with a plan for such diverse issues as breech babies with placenta praevia, left arm weakness with a 10 year history, a splenic abscess, an enormous fibroid uterus, a dislocated shoulder that wasn't, a urethral stricture, a case of HIV related Kaposi's sarcoma, hydronephrotic kidneys, a tuberculous spine and the most vexing problem of 'cracked feet!' It certainly keeps you on your clinical toes! In fact, we had four functioning doctors in action today, so the queue was processed by about 4:30pm.

I was looking forward to another competitive game of pool volleyball when, as seems to be the pattern, an emergency case was carted in. This was tragic. A young man who had been quarrelling with someone at home and decided that the only option was to go out and hang himself. His brother found him and cut him down - still alive and got him to the hospital. Here was this patient, unconscious, reactive pupils, normal pulse, blood pressure, oxygen saturation and blood sugar but complete flaccid paralysis of all four limbs and doubt about the stability of his cervical spine. I wouldn't have been surprised if he had pithed himself or completely transected his spinal cord as a result of breaking his neck. I suspected that if he survived he may well be quadriplegic. Mercifully his X-rays demonstrated no fracture (there is a little peg of bone called the odontoid process in the second top vertebra of the spine and the classical hanging injury causes this bone to break and irrevocably damage the spinal cord). We planned a careful reassessment in the light of day. Never a dull moment!

Downtime and Supermoon

Well Mr Suicide Attempt made a dramatic recovery overnight. Alert, chirpy and moving all four limbs by morning. There is a social worker here that can see him and offer some kind of help and counselling. It is amazing what the human frame can stand! The weekend had been a first chance for me to unwind and relax a little. After a leisurely tour of the hospital to see everyone, including the babies, the children and the maternity unit, the remainder of Saturday was quiet. I sat in the sun, swam in the pool and went down by the river in the evening for a wander. There was a spectacular sunset so took many photos.

On Sunday, after lunch I went with some of the missionaries to a local village about 6 km away. Life here was extremely primitive. The local people existed on subsistence farming only. There are no shops. There is no need for money. There is neither electricity nor piped water. The folks have no proper clothes to wear, only rags. The houses have virtually no furniture! It seemed grim. Strangely enough the people appeared to be completely happy and content and it was touching to receive a very warm and incredibly polite welcome. A large crowd sat around eager to sing and listen to a presentation of the gospel.

On Sunday night there was great anticipation, mainly amongst the medics who fancied themselves as amateur astronomers awaiting a forthcoming lunar eclipse. A blood moon was the expectation. I did some research to see what the ideal time would be to wake up and try to get some pictures of this momentous event. I reckoned 0215 GMT would be the best time to view so I set my alarm for 4:15am local time. So having set the alarm on my phone I plugged it in to charge overnight. David McAdam was all set to follow the coverage on NASA TV on the internet and he was up half the night. The moon was full and the sky clear at 10pm, however by 2am there was a layer of high cloud and the moon was completely invisible. Frustration! As for me, I woke at 6am, to find daylight and was also frustrated that I had missed my alarm and the eclipse. In fact, I found my phone completely discharged, so the alarm had not gone off. My sorrow turned to joy when I discovered that David had spent half the night awake and saw nothing!

Dipalata

Some 80km North East of Chitokoloki lies Dipalata. There is an active mission station there and a hospital with a midwifery service sustained by a senior Irish midwife called Betty Magennis. Betty has served in Africa for around 50 years. We headed for the airstrip at 7:15am to fly to Dipalata. There is an entirely new hospital building, two wards, a delivery suite, a theatre, a laboratory and some additional accommodation, all built by volunteers from Northern Ireland. I had the honour of performing the first surgery in the new unit and seeing the patients admitted to the nice new beds. These were very plush indeed and, in fact, would be considered very good by UK standards. From my experience they were unbelievably good by African standards. The airstrip is a bit rough and ready and has a significant slope at one end. This gives the pilot an interesting set of options when the headwind is barrelling down the up-sloping runway. There was no wind of note today. Just a big thunderstorm! Thunderstorms and flying do not go well together. At lunchtime, as we were entertained to a delicious lunch by the fast talking, diminutive Betty, the thunder rolled and cracked overhead. There wasn't much rain and I think we just caught the edge of the storm. It headed south as we left at 4pm for the short flight back to Chitokoloki. During the 15 minute flight we caught up with the rain but there was no sign of any big thunder clouds. Chris let me fly the plane back to Chitokoloki and he brought us in to land safely and smoothly. This bush flying is a particular skill.

The airstrip is right beside the hospital so it was convenient to drop in to the intensive care area and have a quick look in ICU before sitting out in the setting sun to write this. Our dental abscess patient, who almost lost his life, by now had developed a pyopneumothorax (an enormous collection of infected fluid in this chest cavity) and will need a chest drain placed. A young lady, admitted as a result of acute bleeding from oesophageal varices caused by portal hypertension, in turn as a result of schistosomiasis, is managing to walk around despite a haemoglobin level of 4.2 g / dL. The young girl post resection of an ameloblastoma – (an upper jaw tumour) is much less swollen, sitting up and managing to smile.

The rain storm brought the temperature down to a very pleasant 25 degrees C so everyone was pleased about that.

There are some days in Africa where you would really question whether you made much of a contribution. A subsequent trip to Dipalata gave rise to one of those days. On this occasion five of us set off by road in a hardy Isuzu truck. It normally takes about 15 minutes by air. By road, it is a different story entirely. We spent two hours bouncing and sliding along sandy tracks; deepy rutted in places and having to dodge people, ox carts and a very occasional car coming the other way. The road took us past village after village of basic African dwellings. Sometimes, there would be only about six tiny houses made of mud brick and thatch. None of them has any plumbing and they make do without water, sewage or power. It must be like living in a seriously broken down garden shed with all the contents taken out and thrown away. All the cooking is done outside over a fire. There seem to be children everywhere. If ever one required evidence to support the population projections for the continent of Africa, it is abundant wherever you look. The children were indisputably poverty stricken, always barefoot and dressed in filthy rags. There are occasional exceptions in that some people are dressed well and in nice clothes but they are in a tiny minority.

Betty now has the assistance of a clinical officer who has the most basic of training. On my last visit, we had a few minor surgical cases in children and one in an adult. I was able to take a medical student through some simple suturing and helped her perform her first ever surgical procedure. This may be a boost for her CV if not her confidence! The only other contribution I was able to make was to help Betty, who has spent 5 decades in Zambia, to set up her new computer and get it connected to the mission Wi-Fi network. Now she has Skype, email and WhatsApp so at least that was a good result.

After the two hours' return trip on the excuse for a road, I felt like I had been in a tumble drier. It was always good at the end of a testing day to have some peace and quiet. As I reflected on the fact that I have spent a very limited time in Chitokoloki, it just emphasises the degree of commitment and sacrifice made by the full time missionaries.

Google it!
I led a teaching session for the staff again and this time the topic

was fluid and electrolyte balance. This was a follow-on from the post-operative cardiovascular and respiratory monitoring session. Some of the teaching is only of academic interest here. Since we cannot measure electrolytes or renal function, there is no practical application. Nevertheless, it was a useful session emphasising the clinical issues relating to water and electrolyte balance. We again tried to encourage the nurses to be more diligent. Actually in this regard it would sometimes be hard for them to be less diligent!

In theatre there was another assortment of patients; varices for banding, various wounds and infections, a sumptuous lunch and real difficulty getting motivated for the afternoon.

The plans for pool volleyball were yet again rudely interrupted by the arrival of an ambulance from Lukulu, which is some way south of here in the Western Province. The passenger was a lady in labour. Her first two babies had died. Then she had had three Caesarian sections. Despite this, the doctor at her local hospital had decided that a trial of labour was appropriate! She got to, roughly, the mid-way point of labour then stopped progressing so the conclusion was that she needed a section but that couldn't be done in Lukulu because they had no blood, so she was unceremoniously shipped to Chitokoloki. We had no blood either! Anyway soon after arrival we took her to theatre, a section was done and a little girl arrived safely. The section was tricky with lots of adhesive changes from her previous surgery. David was 'supervising' the anaesthesia and fell asleep at the controls. It is unusual to have both the anaethetist and the patient fast asleep! As I look back I see that I wrote the following in my blog. *Managed to fit in a close game of pool volleyball followed by pizza and brownies and now relaxing and catching up with Facetime contacts. Think I'll dump Facebook though - total waste of time!'*

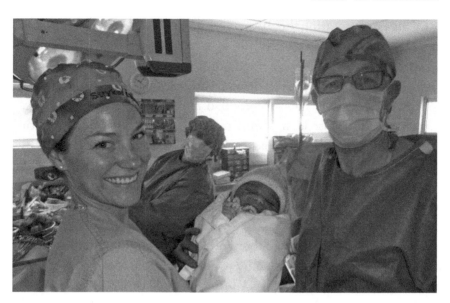

We planned two firsts for the hospital the following day - a peritoneo-venous shunt for refractory ascites and a thoracoscopic sympathectomy for hyperhidrosis. For those who want to know more – Google it!

'Where's Kayumbo?'

There is a certain dynamic in the operating theatre – and whenever anything is required or a question is posed it is not unusual to hear the clarion call: "Kayumbo!" Typically he will suddenly appear at a nearby door with: a huge smile on his face and a "Yes Doc!" Kayumbo is the person who really makes everything happen; he sterilises instruments, prepares packs, sets up all the theatre machinery, knows where everything is, translates, gets consent, lifts patients, and basically runs everything apart from doing the surgery. So what's the problem? The problem was Kayumbo had just gone on holiday for a month! The result - utter chaos. It is not good for this place to be any more chaotic than usual.

Of the two operating theatres, only one can use the air conditioning at any one time. It is very hot to work without it. I think that gynaecology probably won the day for the discipline with the most significant cases. Cervical cancer, ovarian cancer and endometrial cancer all featured. There were also about a dozen minor issues ranging from minor lumps and bumps to a medical examination in another young 12 year old girl allegedly sexually assaulted by the local witch doctor. He threatened to bewitch her if she didn't go with him. The people here see the danger of bewitching as very real and they are scared rigid of such a threat.

Clouds are beginning to gather and the temperature building up in advance of the 'rains.' Hopefully, we'll get a downpour to clear the air and get rid of the ever present distant smell of wood-smoke. The local people seem to burn all the dead vegetation everywhere you look and the result is a constant faint haze. I received the news that there are apparently some oddball cases on their way from both Lusaka and Lolomo so that will likely make up the more interesting surgical activity next week. We also have a prisoner with pathologically sweaty hands, a condition called hyperhidrosis which, when severe, is an extremely uncomfortable and disabling affliction. I plan to divide his thoracic sympathetic chain with the new laparoscopic kit we have. Hopefully, it will cure the patient and get minimal access surgery up and running here. I have been asked to teach twice in the various church services this weekend so important to set aside time for preparation.

Surgacy

The tragedy of poor ante-natal care is in evidence everywhere. The women who deliver babies at home are prone to running into life-threatening problems. Those who have prolonged labour are at real risk of damaging the tissues in the pelvic floor and for some of these women they will end up with a vesico-vaginal fistula. This is a disaster we rarely, if ever, see in the West. The result is that the woman becomes incontinent of urine and constantly leaks through the abnormal connection or fistula that results from the baby's head being stuck in the pelvis for a long period, impairing the local blood supply and resulting in the damage. These women are often rejected by their husbands and are consigned to an unsupported life, stinking of urine and utterly miserable. No one has any clear idea of the fistula burden around the country. I have seen six such cases in only a few weeks here. Many can be helped by surgery although the operations can be complex and specialised.

Rose was such a case. Fortunately, although she came all the way from Angola, I am glad to say that her husband faithfully stood by her and supported her. She was here with him and their two year old son. He was a lovely wee boy - I got a series of high fives every morning. Previous attempts to solve her problem had failed and she suffered difficult complications. Her fistula had involved both bladder and bowel. Now there is just the matter of the complex bladder fistula to repair and a specialist surgeon who is planning to visit in several months will operate on a series of such cases. Despite her problems, Rose is a gentle soul with a ready smile and is very grateful for the help she received even although she has had to be here in Chitokoloki for more than two years already!

There is another remarkable woman here - breast feeding two new-born babies. Every baby is breast-fed. There are few alternatives. This lady is feeding her own baby and the baby born to her sister in law. The sister-in-law died during labour but the baby survived so this lady took on responsibility for feeding both. Amazing!

There is yet another woman who suffered a cardiovascular collapse from blood loss during delivery and almost died. She did survive but unfortunately lost the function of her pituitary meaning, among other things, that she is unable to lactate. So what to do? In the West we would buy some milk formula, a sterilizer, some bottles and solve the problem. None of these are available in this part of rural Africa. The excellent local solution was to buy her a goat to provide milk to feed the baby. No powdered rubbish and all the paraphernalia - just a goat.

I had planned a day of preparation, catching up with email, listening to the internet radio and generally relaxing. But the hospital work just doesn't go away. David McAdam was unwell with malaria so out of commission for a few days. I ended up with an emergency laparotomy for pelvic inflammatory disease yesterday and another acute abdomen with a big intra-abdominal abscess today. Finally finished up about 2pm, prepared my talks and had dinner with a lovely American couple who made fajitas and cake for about 10 of us. Another highlight of the evening was the arrival of Chris, the pilot who arrived from Lusaka with 4 fresh grapefruit for me. That's my vitamin C sorted till I get back to Scotland.

Sepsis
What a weekend! Thunderstorms here can provide an amazing spectacle. The sound of torrential rain and maybe even hail on a corrugated iron roof is deafening.

There is a young man called Emmanuel who has occupied the first bed in the male ward at Chitokoloki for the last 5 or 6 years. He is a great character and despite his lengthy hospitalisation he remains cheerful and willing to take on all-comers who might like to risk challenging him to a game of chess. He sustained a fracture of his cervical spine and has quadriplegia as a result. During his stay he developed about the biggest intra-abdominal abscess I have ever seen. He required an emergency laparotomy to get rid of the infection and following surgery the poor soul was so septic that it was a struggle to maintain his circulation and his blood pressure. I agreed to share his one to one monitoring overnight with Julie Rachel so I wrote this whilst sitting in theatre (Sunday 9pm) waiting for him to breathe on his own. Sepsis can be a killer and at one point he was in serious danger of losing his life. I spent half the night in theatre watching and waiting – it felt like the graveyard shift.

Emmanuel remained ventilator dependent until about 3am when he regained a measure of consciousness and started breathing on his own. It was possible and safe to remove his endo-tracheal tube at 7am. It was a long night. Came back to the house and went to bed for a few hours. Felt rough for most the next day. The lack of energy was probably as much to do with the heat inside and out - there was no escape.

Tomorrow is a holiday - apparently it is Teachers Day! Ha! They seem to have all sorts of days like this. Farmers Day, Youth Day, Ladies Day, Heroes Day. Sounds like any excuse for a day off work! Anyway, one advantage is that there is no clinic in the Old Hospital tomorrow. Several of us were invited to one of the missionary houses for lunch. It turned out to be one of life's more memorable experiences. Apart from sweet potatoes cooked with orange the remainder of the dishes were, in effect, inedible. Our hostess had got hold of some local cow ribs and cooked them. It was the ultimate redefinition of 'dry and chewy,' the meat was the toughest beef I have ever encountered. She said it was an experiment and no doubt it was a well-intentioned experiment. Even with a so-called 'sharp' steak knife I could barely make an impression on these ribs. The consistency was that of a tractor tyre. I didn't have much of an appetite when I arrived and such as it was, it dissipated pretty quickly after an attempt on the ribs.

There was a plan for a plane trip to Chavuma but because we needed shifts of people to monitor our critically ill patient it had to be cancelled. Sometimes there are just not enough people to do all that needs to be done.

The other frustration relates to the internet connection which is patchy at best and occasionally the link drops out altogether. The problem appears to have affected all the access points around the area. In many ways having the internet has made a huge difference to being here and being connected in this way has allowed me to keep track of the developments at home. As it happened my younger daughter Jenni required fairly urgent surgery and being unable to provide any close support I sat under my mosquito net feeling a bit isolated and concerned for her. All I could do was hope and pray for a good outcome.

One dry hand

So, apart from teaching Kayumbo to use a dry razor, I reckon I may have made another contribution to Chitokoloki Mission Hospital today. David McAdam called it a historic day. There were two reasons - first we accomplished the first minimal access operation here and second the operation itself was unusual to say the least. It would even be unusual in the developed world. With a little technical difficulty owing to the lack of a functioning camera and screen I was able to carry out a left thoracoscopic sympathectomy for the man who suffered terrible hyperhidrosis of the hands. The view was suboptimal but the sympathetic chain was easy enough to identify and I had a good enough view to divide it together with the associated lateral branches at the T2 and T3 level. While the patient is anaesthetised it is not possible to assess the adequacy of the operation. However, once back in the ward, we had a happy patient with a working chest drain, a clammy moist right hand and a bone dry left hand. Result! The plan was to do the other side as a subsequent procedure. Having your chest opened on both sides and having to rely on the Chitokoloki post-operative care seemed a little too risky!

Happily I am now legally registered with the Health Professions Council of Zambia but on my first visit I was flying under the radar to some extent. The community is so remote that there are rarely any visits from the hospital inspectors. One day as I was operating, who should show up but the regulators? There was gathering anxiety as we had hoped to finish the case and clear off before the planned hospital inspection. It might have been embarrassing for the local staff to have an unofficial visitor operating in theatre, especially if the Department of Immigration were snooping around or involved. I asked David whether I should make myself scarce but he was totally relaxed about it and so I carried on operating. The inspectors came into the department and even right to the theatre door. I gave them a cheery wave, which was warmly returned, and they went on their way. So much for careful quality control.

What a tip!
I had to make the rather uncomfortable road trip to Zambezi to the nearest immigration office to renew my visa. I was driven there in an elderly Toyota HiLux by Mr David Katota. I had to be reminded by a careful tutorial from the team to remember to indicate that the purpose of my trip was to visit and not to work. Well technically that is correct notwithstanding the fact that I have worked every single day since I got here. However for the purposes of the immigration office and my visa I went for the interview and got the necessary stamp on my passport extending my stay for another 10 days. The road to Zambezi was up to the typical standard - not a trip I would care to use for daily commuting. It was the standard of a rough forest

track and I dread to think what it must be like when the rainy season comes - it will be treacherous. About two-thirds of the distance was on this track. We saw only two other vehicles on the track all day. The remainder of the trip was on a proper black top tarmacadam road. Zambezi itself appears to have little to commend it. It is a most unattractive place. There are higgledy-piggeldy buildings, many of them unfinished or partly broken down. The official immigration office was a desk in a bare room where a man with a uniform and official cap ruled the roost. About the time I was there, Jenni was in the Edinburgh Royal Infirmary being subjected to surgery in a rather more sophisticated health care system - thankfully. You wouldn't want to get sick out here!

David suggested a visit to the provincial government hospital. Many patients are referred to Chitokoloki from here. There was no sign of a doctor. There were a few nurses and the wards were in a sorry state. The best equipped section was the laboratory. It is little wonder that patients request transfer to Chitokoloki because you'd be tempting fate being looked after in a place like this. In fact during my visit, there was a young man who had had inappropriate surgery there being manhandled into a wagon to be transferred to Chitokoloki.

Across the road from the hospital there was a shopping area and market where loads of tomatoes were for sale together with sundry other odds and ends. The stall holders were a cheerless lot. Mind you, I would be grumpy too if I lived in a half-horse town like this. There were various other businesses, not one with an air of prosperity and it was sad to to see the general state of the place. Many of the young men about town had a kind of swagger and some were sporting very noticeable bling. If this is typical of rural Zambian urban living, it is awful. I was glad to leave and drive back through the bush to

Chitokoloki – my bones seriously rattled in a most uncomfortable journey. A highlight was to connect and receive a text from Jenni from her hospital bed in Edinburgh to say that all had gone well.

Frustration

They were there again - the usual queue of hopeful patients waiting to see if their turn would come for surgery today. They come fasted, prepared to sit in the heat all day long. Eventually, if it becomes clear that they will not make the theatre list for that day, they are sent back to the Old Hospital or to their village only to return again on the next operating day.

Today we really only managed one significant case. I took a pyonephrotic kidney out of a six month old baby. The surgery was the easiest part. The anaesthetic was much more eventful. Despite his chronic renal sepsis, this wee guy was of the slightly chubby variety, at least his limbs were. I think the best term would be 'pudgy.' Consequently, peripheral veins were not plentiful and were very tricky to canulate. With the help of the ultrasound machine attempts were made to get into his external jugular - no joy. We finally got the internal jugular vein and after nearly two hours of fiddling and faffing David managed to get him off to sleep and paralysed. At operation he had a grossly enlarged and infected left kidney with an obvious hydroureter all the way down to his bladder base. When the kidney was fully mobilised it became obvious that he had not one but two hydro-ureters on that side so a congenital anomaly with a duplex system. That was probably part of the reason that the system became infected in the first place - almost certainly he had obstruction at the vesico-ureteric junction. The surgery took about 45 minutes. Waking him up took the rest of the day; at least until 3pm. In the course of waking him up it became clear that the internal jugular line had leaked and the hunt for an alternative site was on again. I even made a cut down on the ankle and found a pathetic scrawny long saphenous vein. It was impossible to canulate it even with the vein open before my eyes! We eventually managed to get into a scalp vein. The line was stitched in securely and he was returned to his mum and to ICU. I really hope he'll be OK. There is not much room for manoeuvre with such a tiny character.

The second case planned for the day was our jailbird who needed the second side of his thoracic sympathectomy completed. As we sent for him, the news came back that he had just had his 'nshima!' This is the bulky tasteless dough which has almost no nutritional value so far as I can see. It is, however, what the locals eat every day. I doubt that a roast suckling pig would even compete for a place on their menu. If they have not had their nshima, they consider that they have not eaten. Given that fasting is considered an essential preparation for general anaesthesia, a dose of this stuff was not such a great idea. The conspiracy theorists reckon that it was a deliberate ploy on the part of the patient to delay his operation and prolong his stay in the relatively luxurious surroundings of the men's ward; certainly luxurious in comparison to the local prison. He probably doesn't fancy going back to having the living day lights beaten out of him on a regular basis. The plan? Try again the following morning!

We still had no internet and everyone was complaining. However Chris the pilot was in Lusaka and transported a satellite technician back with him to get it sorted out. So hope springs that tomorrow may see us all reconnected.

Success and profound sadness
The final few days of my first visit to Chitokoloki were peppered with mixed emotions. We finally managed to tackle the other side

of the planned bilateral thoracoscopic sympathectomy and what a struggle it turned out to be. There was a leak from the insufflator so it was difficult to get satisfactory collapse of the right lung to deflect it out of the way. I had thought the right chest would have been easier because there is less in the way (e.g. the heart) and it is generally easier to collapse the right lung and push it out of the way. With the intrathoracic pressure at atmospheric levels, the lung was not for co-operating. I struggled a bit finding only fleeting glimpses of what I thought was the sympathetic chain. When you have a clear view it is usually not too difficult to positively identify the subtle autonomic nerve chain as it courses over the necks of the ribs. With all the manipulation the pleura was beginning to become reddened making visualisation even more difficult. Eventually when we sorted out the gas supply the elation was short lived as the light source then failed as a result of overheating! Typical! As they say here, often in exasperation, 'This is Africa.' When the light rebooted, I was able to identify the chain and get a power source connected to burn it decisively over the necks of the second and third ribs. Three hours later in the ward - two dry hands. Persistence in the face of adversity had paid off!

Later that day I was called back urgently as a little girl from a village some 5km away had been brought in unconscious following a snake bite. There are basically three categories of snake bites. Some are neurotoxic and cause paralysis (cobra and mamba), others are cytotoxic (e.g. puff adder) causing enormous local tissue damage and others are haemotoxic. This affects the blood; these are the snakes that typically bite then hold on and inject venom from their posterior fangs.

Apparently this 8 year old girl was bitten at about 8am and she was initially weak, taken home and given some village medicines.

Goodness only knows what she was given but it was completely useless. She finally arrived at the hospital, moribund. This was desperate. All attempts to resuscitate her, including intubation of her airway and cardiac massage, failed. It was too late. She was declared dead at 12:30pm. If she had been taken to the hospital (a 10 minute ambulance ride) earlier she could almost certainly have been saved. When I saw her, she had fixed dilated pupils and there was virtually no hope. It was most likely a neurotoxic venom from a mamba or the like. When the story emerged from the family it also turned out that it had been her elder brother who had been taken and killed by a crocodile in the river some 4 weeks before. It was just such an unbelievable tragedy for that family.

Chinyingi!

One of the most unsettling experiences of my time in Africa occurred today. I had been expecting a slow day and once again I was proved wrong. A patient with an ectopic pregnancy punctuated the early afternoon. I attempted a laparoscopic approach but again had some difficulties with the insufflator. That plan was abandoned and instead we resorted to an old fashioned open operation.

David McAdam has been keen to take a few of us to one of the only local attractions, the Chinyingi Bridge. This is a suspension footbridge across the Zambezi. It was built in the 70s by local Catholic missionaries in response to a boating tragedy many years ago. A mercy mission in a monk's boat making a trip from Chinyingi to the town of Zambezi was lost in the river on the return journey and went down with the loss of several people on board. The missionary concerned researched bridge building and went on to acquire material from the mines in the copper belt and other sundry suppliers of wire, cable and concrete and proceeded to build what amounted to a home made suspension bridge. Our plan was to arrive just before sunset. In fact, we arrived in total darkness some 20 minutes after sunset. It took about an hour and a half on the very bumpy dirt roads to get there. The bridge stretched out over the river Zambezi that at a guess would be about 300 yards wide at this point. I confess I was a little nervous about making my way across this dangerous river on a dodgy home-made bridge. However, since we had taken the trouble to get there it would have seemed churlish not to venture across even although I could not see my hand in front of my face!

There was nothing else for it but to step forth into the darkness (all the while thinking that this is likely far from safe even in daylight, never mind total darkness). The bridge was wide enough only for single file. It bounced and shuddered, swayed and swung. We crossed all the way and then headed back. The hand-rail was not visible in the dark but felt like it had been fashioned from twisted barbed wire. Never was I so glad as to arrive back beside the car. David spared us the tales of various incidents where people have put their foot through the bridge and ended up in the river below. The river looks innocuous enough - it's just that the inhabitants are more of a threat, whether the schistosomes or the crocodilians. I escaped with a few mosquito bites.

It was good to have a subsequent quiet day. Time for reading and reflection. I decided to read the acclaimed 'Life of Pi' by Yann Martel. In my view it is utter garbage but quite well written and good for a few choice quotes which I have noted.

The kidney baby developed acute gastric retention and this will hold up his recovery for a few days. Despite being told not to feed him, his mother was breast feeding as normal. The poor wee chap was unable to process it and developed aspiration pneumonia as a result. However, his mother has been severely reprimanded and he has progressed well today.

A retired American surgeon and his wife, Kevin and Lesley Kerrigan, have been here to help for the last couple of weeks. It has been an absolute pleasure to get to know them and work with them. They come from Spokane in Washington. They have worked as a team and because there are two visiting surgeons we have been able to run clinics and sometimes two theatre lists concurrently. Kevin has had a lot of prior African experience in parts of Ethiopia and Rwanda.

Kevin, Lesley and I survived the Chinyingi Bridge trip together. It is a pity there was no tee shirt stall selling: "I survived the Chinyingi Bridge." We would all have bought one. Actually there was no stall - no nothing. For a bridge that featured in the 'National Geographic' magazine a few years ago it would potentially be a good tourist attraction. The chance of such a development here - zero!

Come to think of it, since coming here I have not spent one single kwacha. There are some shops but not shops that you would ever want to buy anything from. Occasionally, someone arrives with a few bottles of cold Coke or Sprite from a stall near the hospital entrance. The cost is very low. The bottles are recycled and it emphasises why the three words common to virtually every language are: 'hallelujah' 'amen' and 'Coca-Cola!'

The following day, Kevin took one of the local nurses to Chavuma Mission Hospital to do some cases there. The plane takes about 35 minutes and it is important to carry everything that is needed. As well as Chris the pilot, the internet technician from Lusaka was also making the trip. That was a full load for the petite Cessna.

Pound of flesh.

This has been an intense experience. Culturally, this place is shocking in so many ways. The local people live a curious life. It is incongruous that many have mobile phones while the living accommodation is the way it has been here for many hundreds of years. 'Primitive' doesn't begin to describe it. No power. No water. No furniture. No protection from common diseases. Numerous cases of advanced exotic conditions that are never seen in the West. And dangers; malaria, bilharzia, HIV, snakes, crocodiles, village medicines and witch doctors!

I will likely have a short fuse in future for people who moan about the NHS. What a contrast! We have access to free, high quality, specialist care, delivered by trained professionals in clean hospitals with sterilised equipment. People in the UK moan about having to wait to be seen or maybe even having to lie on a trolley for a while. At least they can be seen within a few hours. Here, they may have to walk or be carried by friends with a bike or an ox cart for days or weeks to get to a hospital like Chitokoloki to have a chance to see a doctor. In the UK, suspected cancer is dealt with quickly and while people whose joints wear out may have to wait for a few months to have a new joint, in rural Africa there is virtually no chance of joint replacement. Even if there was the possibility of such a procedure, the conditions are such that the chances of the new joint swimming in infection within a few days would be unacceptably high.

I did a little survey with the help of one of the visiting medical students. I already mentioned the real risks of anaemia and while we saw occasional patients with dangerously low blood counts it has been amazing to me that people here seem to survive with blood counts which would have doctors concerned and arranging emergency specialist referrals in the UK or the USA. We were keen to note the haemoglobin levels in our ward population. Given that the normal range for adults is 12.5 g/dL to around 15.5g/dL we checked the haemoglobin levels for all the patients in the hospital on one particular day. The average level for the adult wards was almost identical for the male and female side at 7.4 and 7.5g/dL respectively. For the children's ward, it was 8.3g/dL. Anyone in my practice at home with a level of 8 or less would be prescribed 2 or 3 units of blood. So why not give them blood here? Simple, there is none. Chris took a picture of the allocation for the whole country of Zambia last week during a trip to Lusaka. There were about 22 packs of blood. The Chitokoloki share? 4 units! Totally inadequate. So why not just get local donors? It's illegal! I will say more about this later but it amounts to a totally insane policy. The Americans are partly to blame in as much as this is represents an unintended consequence of some rules they insisted upon in exchange for the generous funding provided to set up a state of the art transfusion service. The conditions were that every donation of blood had to be tested for HIV, Hepatitis B and C amongst other transmissible viruses. Then the government had to outlaw local donations which were not screened in this way. The result is that any blood given, other than in the central blood transfusion centre e.g. by relatives or volunteers to help a dying patient, is against the law. Some laboratory staff have been fined or even fired in some places. Our team in Chitokoloki are so scared to go against this policy that it has become very difficult even to use blood that is known to come from a safe source. So a few patients are spared the risk of catching Hepatitis C whilst thousands die of acute anaemia or blood loss. Nuts!

Another good example as to why politicians should be kept a country mile away from healthcare!

Anyway, I'm away to pack my bags. Chris is planning for 'wheels up' (pilot speak) at 9:30am. David wants me to go to the hospital at 7:30am and show him how to put in a peritoneo-venous shunt for ascites. Hence the 'pound of flesh' reference. I'm coming home for a rest!

Africa again – 2016

In August 2016, I had the amazing privilege of visiting Chitokoloki again. Jenni came as well so while this was a second visit for both of us it was the first chance to go together. A father and daughter medical adventure - not to be missed!

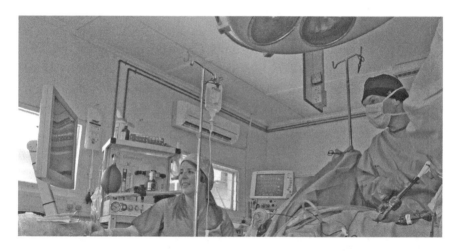

Back of beyond

We arrived in Lusaka and made our way to the Flight House where we had accommodation booked as we passed through on our way to Chit. It is very comfortable and we met some old friends from previous trips. We also made some new friends with people variously involved in aviation and logistics support as we set up the travel plans for our first day. It was great to catch up with Chris Brundage the pilot.

The game plan was to head to Chitokoloki aboard the Cessna 206 with two other passengers (Marion Ronald and Betty Magennis); one for Loloma and one for Dipalata. Both of the senior lady missionaries, on being introduced to Jenni, asked her if she was a nurse! This provided just a frisson of mild frustration but fortunately a very kind and gentle response from Jenni to explain her actual role as a qualified doctor.

However, by the time we were organised to leave Lusaka, time was tight and with sunset at 6.15pm we were only able to fly as far as Loloma. We came in to land after a two and a half hour flight having seen very little on the way. The route was over bush and swamp for most of the way and with all the traditional burning of vegetation it was almost impossible to make out the details of the ground from 10,500 feet. These were really instrument flying conditions for most of the journey. About an hour out of Lusaka (where we took off right after the arrival of today's massive Emirates 777-300) the radio became silent. Despite the approaching sunset, I was surprised at how high the sun appeared to be. However, it drops quickly and with almost no twilight it rapidly became pitch dark.

One advantage of the forced layover was the chance to visit the Loloma Mission Hospital and connect again with Dr Joel Nkonde, the single handed doctor we had met on a previous visit. He gave us a tour. He is a bit like a GP but provides much of the maternity care and even does some fairly adventurous surgery in limited resource conditions. The place appears to be a hotch-potch of random buildings. I quickly became disorientated as he took us through the various wards. We saw some desperate cases. One poor chap with about 30% burns. He was in desperate need of dressings and grafting but was lying on a mattress on a filthy floor under a grubby blanket; his wounds were otherwise exposed and he was in severe pain. He was fairly stoic about it but when we saw the state of his leg, the blood supply to his lower left leg was so badly damaged that his foot was already gangrenous. Unfortunately, his fate had been sealed.

We also saw a 65 year old man with a curious necrotising infection around his left knee. He told me a story of some 20 years of pain likely due to TB in his spine. As for his leg, there is very little option to provide skin cover because he is so thin. The wound badly needs debridement. He should probably get to Chitokoloki where there is at least some chance of maybe sparing him an above knee amputation.

We also saw two children with forearm fractures - one who had spiral fractures of both radius and ulna from falling out of a tree. The other was a typical greenstick fracture; the type that is quite common in young children. There were also patients with femoral fractures in traction. There were two adults with meningococcal meningitis and both seemed to be responding well to antibiotics. In addition, there were plenty of maternity and paediatric cases. Many of the children had malnutrition, some had gastroenteritis and fevers and there was one wee lad who had severe anaemia (haemoglobin of 3.0g/dL) despite having already had two units of blood. One of the missionaries (Joy Beers) gave a further unit at the hospital before returning to her house to serve us dinner. Despite having their own family of three children plus a colleague they seemed to effortlessly entertain the five of us from the aircraft. Very impressive!

Conversations at dinner ranged from medical disasters to local wildlife. The stories were of tiger fish, traffic hazards, various nasty snakes and a few other adventures. Everyone was complaining of the cold - the temperature drops to about 10 degrees C at night-time. Usually in Scotland if we get as high as 12 degrees it's almost cause for celebration.

Welcome back

What a place! Loloma is in the middle of nowhere. Out here in the bush everyone was wrapped up for winter. It was good to get some sleep but I found myself awake at about 2 am and again at about 4 am. The reason? Crazed roosters that have no idea of the rules! They are supposed to crow at dawn. There seemed to be an army of them here crowing away virtually all night long. That along with what sounded like a distant but loud energetic radio broadcast or PA announcement of some sort. It was possibly something to do with upcoming elections. Apparently there was a lot at stake. If the current President was not successful in being re-elected it was considered likely that he would end up in jail. It seems that they not infrequently have the election rallies and announcements in the middle of the night. I guess we need to put it down to a cultural difference.

We left Loloma at just after eight and after the cows were chased off the runway we were off. I flew a good chunk of the way to Dipalata where we dropped Betty. She got out of the plane, engine still running, and we were off again to Chitokoloki. Chris was asking on the radio for traffic information - silence! Inbound to Chitokoloki we followed a flood plain down to an intersect with the Zambezi and Chris then flew us along the river at about 30 feet above the water for about 5 miles.

There were tales of locals being spooked by this low flying malarkey and diving for cover or even jumping out of their dug out canoes into the water for fear of the plane colliding with them! Having roared across the mission station, we flew a circuit and landed to be

met by Gordon Hanna and Joey and Kaitlin Speichinger. They have just adopted a Zambian baby whose 17 year old mother died of a major haemorrhage during labour. The father and family didn't want the child so they have taken this wee boy into their family. They've called him Owen.

Our arrival was carefully timed to coincide with tea-break! Jenni was convinced that she was going to have to play the role of housekeeper - I was confident that the level of service I enjoyed before, courtesy of the mysterious Mary, might be on offer again. We have been allocated the duplex as our house and Mary was there to meet us. A freshly made pizza was in the fridge, the larder stacked with more than enough food and a huge variety so Jenni was suitably impressed. Topping it off was an invitation to the Hannas for lunch so we have been royally received and entertained.

Having unloaded our bags from the aircraft we went to the hospital. Jenni got involved in dressings and sedation for some of the burns patients and then came in to help in theatre. David McAdam was doing a difficult cataract and I started with an open prostate, then after lunch, an emergency hysterectomy for a perforated uterus and then a very difficult intestinal case they had been saving up for me. This was a desperately malnourished woman; as thin an adult as I have ever seen. She had an ileostomy that was pouring fluid and electrolytes and causing her severe dehydration and really threatening her survival. An operation to close her stoma was a last ditch attempt to save her life. They had attempted this nearly three months ago and abandoned the case because of adhesions and difficulty. She had lost a lot of ground since then. We made good progress and after some very tentative dissection for fear of damaging things further it proved possible to find two good sections of bowel and put them back together again. Hopefully, she will be able to have enough reserve to heal and avoid any nasty complications.

This evening we went to the Bible study and had a session on 2 Corinthians 2 before coming back to deal with emails, demolish the pizza, take our doxycycline and write this.

Hoping for the lack of nocturnal rooster activity tonight!

Medical heresy

After an early start this morning we attended the weekly teaching session. This was well attended by doctors, nurses, care assistants, pharmacists and even the social worker and was followed by a visit to the overcrowded ICU. There were about 9 patients in various stages of decrepitude - some poor souls in a really bad way. I feel really sorry for the burns patients. They have little chance of good recovery and will be terribly scarred. We have seen several small children with nasty burns. One lad will need his right arm amputated within a day or two because the hand and forearm were dead following the burn injury. Jenni and I did a hysterectomy for an early cancer during the morning. David's son JP gave the spinal, which was slow to work and eventually had to be topped up with a general anaesthetic. The patient was oblivious to David's demand that she 'go to sleep' and 'stop moving - ridiculous!' Anyhow we eventually had good enough anaesthesia to get ahead and remove the offending organ.

A real highlight of working in Chitokoloki is the good natured banter that goes on within the team. I sense that the American sense of humour does not quite resonate with the kind of friendly abuse which is exchanged between the Scots and the Irish. The discussions were peppered by some disagreement between Jenni and David McAdam. He has a healthy disrespect for much medical dogma and really quite likes winding people up. His ideas about IV fluids (dangerous and overused), blood pressure (hypotension is mostly not relevant), and even oxygen (potentially toxic), all provoked the desired reaction of incredulity from those who were younger and considered themselves wiser! And they all took the bait!

When we came back to the house feeling rather worn out, Jenni was delighted and slightly embarrassed that the amazing Mary had done all her laundry!

I managed to get a FaceTime call to my dad – truly amazing technology. Too bad it was not available when Frederick Stanley Arnot and George Suckling established this mission back in 1914 – it may have been an entirely different enterprise. My dad who is now in his 96th year is totally amazed that we can make video calls for no additional cost! The down side it that he now has to ask Alexa to pause while he connects! It looked sunny in Scotland and while it is winter here, it is still hot during the day.

Today's horror story - it was really the lunchtime entertainment. Apparently one of the workers found a 9 foot black mamba in a store house just beside where the McAdams live. The mamba is one of the world's deadliest snakes. It is said that an adult mamba has enough venom to kill about 20 men. Following a bite the patient becomes paralysed and could be dead within an hour. Amazingly enough, with an injection of anti venom the problem can be very effectively treated such that in a moribund patient breathing can be restored and the patient rendered fit to walk out of hospital in a couple of hours. Anyhow, this large mamba retreated behind some boxes at the back of the small outdoor storehouse. The missionaries decided to empty the boxes one by one to confront the snake. (In the course of this tale I asked how fast and how aggressive these things can be. The answer: 'lighting fast - faster than a galloping horse' and 'very aggressive.' Not sure I want to meet one.) Anyway, the story continued that the snake, having retreated behind the last box, was cornered. Gordon Hanna rapidly removed the last box, ducked and Chris the pilot, ready with his shotgun, blew the monster apart. All a bit dramatic for my liking.

Jenni and I are on guard, every tree root is being regarded with a healthy degree of suspicion especially in the dark!

Wonderdrug

Jenni is compiling a list of medical conditions and practices David McAdam either doesn't believe in or thinks is a waste of time. Allergies, check. ME, for sure. Measuring blood pressure apart from after a spinal – a waste of effort. Giving fluids to burns patients – over-rated and likely dangerous. Giving fluids to any patient especially post-operative patients, – likely unnecessary in most cases. Giving any nutrition to post-op laparotomy patients for several days – forbidden. Most, if not all, of these ideas would be considered heretical. He, however, is totally unrepentant and prepared to argue (maybe just for the fun of it) with anyone who expresses a different view. Jenni is quick to seize the bait and slope off in disgust at the sheer effrontery of it all. David announced to the staff this morning that he was leaving for a month during the next calendar year. The reason: "My son has had the misfortune to find himself a wife!" Actually, he is going to Newfoundland for the wedding. It is quite a hassle to get there. After arrival, there are apparently no hire cars available and with limited options for places to stay he was not happy. In preparation for his departure he worked solidly, with the rest of the team today, to clear as many patients as possible. We have a list on the board showing the patients waiting for surgery so there is plenty to keep us going for the next week or two.

Today, I operated on a thyroid for first time in more years than I can remember. It was straightforward and the patient seemed to recover well. Then we did an old lady (62!) with a big abdominal mass. We thought it was a tumour and so it proved. There was a view that we should leave her to die. However, since she was miserable with chronic obstruction I opened her belly and found a locally advanced but resectable tumour which was removed and reconstructed. This was all accomplished without formal anaesthesia just sedation with ketamine. Absolutely amazing and I am prompted once again to ask: 'Who needs anaesthetists?'

We were then prepared to do an amputation for the wee boy with the burned arm. His father was not willing to consent so we will have to wait until the arm gets worse. The problem is that the gangrene will soon threaten the child's life so we will inevitably end up doing this procedure soon.

We saw a host of new patients with various surgical conditions. It is very difficult to communicate with them without an interpreter. Some have serious problems whereas others are fine and worried about totally minor and irrelevant issues.

Jenni can now apparently hear a mouse in the kitchen - so I am going to sign off and investigate!

Bites

Another first for me today! I saw a patient with a hippopotamus bite! This poor chap who had been blown up some years ago by stepping on a land mine and having lost his right leg proceeded to fashion an artificial leg for himself by moulding melted down plastic containers and forming a replacement limb, complete with a small wooden foot and carved toes. He had been out in his boat and collided with something on the river. Assuming that he was in shallow water and that he had simply run aground he was totally shocked to discover the real reason. A hippopotamus emerged, tipped him out of his boat and as he struck out for the shore the beast bit him on the backside! It took a healthy chunk of tissue. At least it now seems to be healing. On the ward round I also saw a wee lad bitten by a cobra some three days ago. It got him in the hand and his arm was horribly swollen. Fortunately, it looks like it is beginning to improve and he will get away without losing any tissue. As we moved around - there were two other patients suffering the effects of bites (not counting the numerous patients with malaria), one crocodile bite and one human bite resulting in the amputation of the little finger. It occurred to me that life would be much safer if the different species would just refrain from biting one another! It is also true to note that none of the species hereabouts seem to major on dental hygiene.

The hospital work can offer an amazing variety and most of the decision making and even much of the investigative work has to be done as one goes along. There is no real concept of *sending* a patient for an x-ray – it is much more like *taking* the patient, finding the radiographer, assisting with the set up and then reviewing the images afterwards. A similar scenario would apply to a patient who may require a change of dressing. Take the patient to the appropriate place and get on with it!

One afternoon, I returned to the hospital at about 2:45pm to see some patients in the clinic. Some had come for scans, some for consideration for surgery. At that point an emergency case was admitted - a young man with a strangulated hernia. Everything else stopped while we took him off to theatre. Such are the responsibilities that crowd into the available time it was about 7pm before we managed to get him into theatre. Jenni did a spinal anaesthetic and I went ahead with the operation to explore the hernia. Partly as a result of the unintentional delay some of the bowel within the hernia itself was already gangrenous and had to be removed. By far the safest option was to abandon the small local

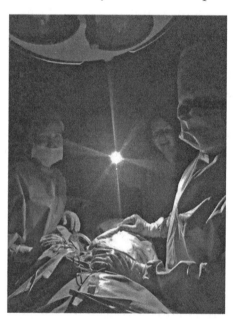

incision and make a proper 'maximal access' operation by means of a laparotomy. This allowed us to sort the problem out by removing the dead bowel and choosing two healthy segments of gut to join together again. This was all fine until we were just about finished and there was an unannounced complete power failure. I was hand tying a suture and we were plunged into the blackest darkness. The contrast to complete darkness was probably accentuated because we had been working under the bright lights. Anyway we completed the operation using the lights from two iPhones! They produced enough light (just) to finish off the procedure. Just as we finished, the generators kicked in and normal service resumed.

The evening was topped off at a barbeque at our neighbours' house. Joey and Kaitlin have a brilliant patio complete with fire pit with a grid for roasting hamburgers, German sausage and potato wedges. Always keen on healthy eating, this was followed by s'mores; big roasted marshmallows and chocolate biscuits. Didn't expect that in a remote corner of Zambia.

Peace

Jenni went in early today and saw all the patients. I arrived about an hour and half later and added my tuppence worth. All the post-op contenders are doing well. Two cases in ITU looked decidedly shaky. One is a young woman who is septic and toxic from some self medication she took in a suicide attempt. She is unconscious, has a high fever, normal blood sugar despite diabetes and appears to have normal renal and liver function. She is distended and oedematous and we really do not know what is going on. The other is an alcoholic man with severe burns and he and the girl are likely not to survive much longer. (They both died in the course of the day.)

We had a fairly quiet day thereafter. We sat outside and read for a while. Jenni and I made a trip to the blue shop and bought a crate of juice to give our visitors - 8 bottles of Coke, 8 of Fanta and 8 of Sprite. We carted the crate back to the house - it seemed a long way with a full crate of juice! We roasted a chicken and cooked some of our spuds to concoct a chicken and broccoli bake followed by home made lemon drizzle cake. Delicious, even although the cake turned out to be nothing much to look at, it tasted fantastic. We had J-R, Christina and Chris join us for dinner. The evening was interrupted by one call from the hospital but nothing desperate so we had a good time chatting and hearing about the details of life and death in Africa!

It is Sunday tomorrow so I have been added to the roster for preaching in the local church. Only a handful of the congregation can really handle English effectively so my Manchester United supporting friend who is also an elder in the local fellowship will be my translator. In the afternoon, we are planning a trip to some of the local villages to present the gospel so that should be interesting. Monday is designated as Farmer's Day and is a public holiday. After that we will be back into action so, bracing ourselves.

Election fever

It was a welcome change to have a relatively quiet weekend. When the work is so relentless it seems to accentuate the need to re-charge and enjoy some 'down-time' occasionally.

That evening we went to the home of Joey and Kate Speichinger for pizza. They are American but have been full time in Africa for several years. Joey is a trained aircraft mechanic and can deal with any mechanical or maintenance problem, whether on aircraft or not. Kate is a nurse and is also incredibly versatile. They are wonderful hosts and offer hospitality to the many guests who come to Chitokoloki despite their other heavy responsibilities. This event was actually a guise for an early birthday celebration for Jenni. They had even made birthday cup cakes and their home was decked out with balloons and banners.

On the holiday Monday, we went to see all the patients and ended up manipulating two fractures, overseeing some dressings and X-rays and Jenni carried out an incision and drainage for a four year old with a big sub-mental abscess. Nasty business! Anyway, the rest of the day and evening we were able to relax and hold ourselves in readiness for a big operating day tomorrow. The schedule starts with an elective section, followed by two or three redo bowel cases they have been storing up for me as well as a thyroglossal cyst. Not sure how far down the list we will get - it just seems to get longer and longer.

Apparently, the President of Zambia is planning to visit Zambezi and Chitokoloki next Sunday. Gordon Hanna has told his political aides that since he is coming to campaign for the election the following week he will not be welcome in the mission or the hospital. It sounds like he might come anyway! The whole election business sounds completely rigged and crooked and the Patriotic Front party has been using taxpayer resources to run their election campaign. Gordon reckons that the opposition party will win as much as 80% of the vote but the sitting government will still manage to cling on to power. No wonder they are expecting trouble. Gordon has informed the President's staff that once he is in government he will be delighted to welcome him to come for tea. However, while he is on a political party campaign - he is not welcome. Not sure I want his autograph. Maybe a selfie and then a retreat to the background. We'll see.

Jenni's birthday.
We all celebrated Jenni's birthday again at tea break in the hospital half way through the morning. J-R had baked a big iced chocolate cake so again we had the candle blowing ceremony!

We operated all day. First, the tricky elective section in a woman who had four kids and three previous Caesarian deliveries. She bled like it was going out of style. Jenni assisted me and helpfully pointed out all the areas of active bleeding that I had thus far failed to control! We got there in the end. A baby girl was safely delivered, the bleeding controlled and both were doing well. Second, a wee five year old - about the same size as Jaz, my grandson. He was a brave wee lad with a very attentive mum. He had had two previous abdominal operations with a colostomy and a mucus fistula. We put him back together again and so this was more in my line of specialty practice, just on a smaller scale! Third - another gut reconstruction for a chap with some kind of stoma. It looked a bit like a narrow colostomy (it turned out that the previous operation note was totally confusing) but when we opened him up it was straightforward to put things to rights. Jenni took out the appendix en passant. Then we had a minor case to finish off. A simple hernia in a young woman. I had examined her in the standing position in the clinic. That is fairly standard for hernias. There was no available couch to lie her down in any event. However when she was given her spinal anaesthetic it became obvious that she had a significant swelling in her lower abdomen - about the size of a 15 week pregnancy. It turned out that a pregnancy test had not been done. Well, we decided to fix her hernia anyway and then scanned her to stage the size of the baby. About 14 weeks on ultrasound. The remainder of the queue were invited to return koomadiki! Tomorrow.

The theatre team at Jenni's birthday tea-break. Kayombo, Womba and Chilanda - brilliant people!

David McAdam had asked me to lead a Bible study on 2 Corinthians 3 so I spent a bit of time preparing and studying the passage. In the end, two people turned up so we decided that it might be better to save the prep and use the material on Sunday. Visited Chris with some of the local staff for a session of Rook and Dobble all frantically and hotly contested.

Happy birthday to Jack!

Clinic day. Actually managed to finally clear the queue by about 4:30pm. The amazing thing about the queue is that no matter how many of you are working and no matter how many patients there are (and there are many) the line never seems to go down. Until finally, there is a noticeable change but only very late in the day when all of a sudden you are left with just one or two and - final triumph! Actually today was punctuated by a few challenging problems. One vesico-vaginal fistula patient had started to leak urine - indicating a failed procedure. One complex intestinal reconstruction started to leak intestinal content through her wound. This was desperately disappointing but not surprising because she has virtually no capacity to heal anything in view of her poor nutritional state. One boy came with terrible burns and I had to amputate four fingers and a thumb. Then it occurred to me that a patient was missing. A lady who had been breast feeding and presented with a breast abscess was supposed to show up for review and she failed to appear. Who knows what happened?

Jenni has figured out the reason why people who don't have much wrong with them generally complain of the same thing. 'I am paining' - the clinical officers have often written 'GBP' - general body pains. A bit like the 'pain all over' brigade in the UK. She thinks it represents the general aches and pains associated with active hard physical work in people who are chronically unwell. She is probably right.

I came back pretty tired and after a couple of FaceTime calls (my father Jack's birthday - he was in very good form) spent the evening reading, answering emails and preparing for the weekend. There will be more surgery tomorrow just the usual stuff in patients with little reserve, no subcutaneous fat, profound anaemia, big spleens and portal hypertension. Apart from that – entirely straightforward!

It would give you the willies

Today's list included a Hartmann's stoma reversal in an HIV positive soldier whose previous attempt at this surgery in May failed when he crashed his blood pressure and had to be resuscitated. We had success this time although it took about three hours and ended up with a technically challenging reconstruction and rather more surgery than we bargained for. Following that, during a laparotomy for a big mobile ovarian dermoid tumour my assistant, a nurse called Womba, nearly keeled over and had to be dragged away from the table before she collapsed. We then had a couple of paediatric cases to do before lunch. One was a jaw biopsy for a big tumour in a three year old. The second was a good natured wee chap of 8 who lost his forearm following a snake bite and he needed a skin graft for his forearm stump. At the prospect of his injection he took a complete flakey, was punching, kicking and screaming. We had to hold him down and shoot some ketamine into his leg and he was sleeping peacefully after about 3 or 4 minutes. After lunch, we did a clutch of other cases, Jenni acting as anaesthetist for some and surgeon for others.

Today, a 55 year old man pitched up unannounced and said he had a nasty wound on his private parts. He took off the dressings giving a story that some eight months before he had been circumcised in a bush hospital in Angola and the wound had been present since that time. He endured a necrotising infective process. It was indurated and tender and the urethra had a clearly identifiable defect. I emailed a photo to some urology colleagues in Glasgow who promptly replied with their advice and answers to my questions.

Should we make any attempt to repair the urethra? If so, with what technique? What about a catheter? What about skin cover as and when the wound is clean and granulating?

Should we graft the area? Perhaps we may need to consider amputation!

To be honest, I remain concerned about recurrent infection - nasty pyogenic infections are incredibly common and troublesome here.

Tomorrow, I have volunteered to go out with 'Sista' Dorothy who looks after all sorts of chronically unwell patients in their communities. She is the American from California who has been here since the early 1990s. She treks out in her battered truck bartering for produce and taking orders for medicines, checking blood pressures and picking up numerous passengers. It sounds like a bit of an adventure. Jenni did this a year or so ago and still bears the scars. I will report back if I survive.

On the road - "PATRICK!"
Well, for me, today was the day spent on the African bush dirt roads and visiting numerous villages. It was truly amazing. The roads are grim and on return I felt like every bone in my body had been shaken up with vigour. Unrelenting bumps, ruts and careering along some thirty degrees off the horizontal is a challenging experience. Dorothy was driving and she has an encyclopaedic knowledge of the local area - by that I mean

villages scattered in an area of perhaps 500 square kilometres and it seems as though everyone knows her! We would be bouncing along some dirt track in the middle of nowhere when she would pull up, blow her horn and within 20 seconds people would start to arrive. Some were patients. Some were curious bystanders.

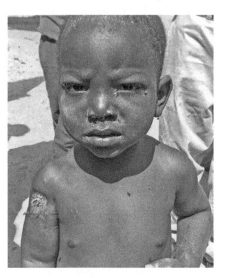 About 90% were children, mostly under 7. Dorothy then dispensed the required medication to tide them over for the next two months. She must have seen about 25 or 30 patients. On occasion, I got out and examined a chest, listened to a heart or had a prod at an abdomen. At some stops (of which there were many) I took blood pressures on arms that were thrust into the car. At one stop I had a kick about with some talented local lads with impressive ball skills despite playing in their bare feet. One stop involved Dorothy visiting a 'pit' - a bathroom break. I had had breakfast then no food or water until my return at 5pm. No pit for me! Every time the car stopped Dorothy had asked her worker Patrick to jump out of the back of the car and come to her window. She was keen to do as much of this itinerant chronic disease clinic from the driver's seat as possible. She seemed to be irritated when she had to get out. Sometimes Patrick would not appear. She would yell - "Patrick" - and as if by magic he was at her side: "Yes Madam!" Poor Patrick had to ride in the back with about 8 others and all the sacks, bags and luggage including a paraplegic man who was nearly buried by all the stuff that had been accumulated.

We delivered 5 patients from hospital back to their communities. They rode in the back of her Isuzu truck. I was in the relative comfort of the front seat. In absolute terms there was no comfort. Those in the back had no cushioning and some were quite frail. Having gone out with a load, we returned with a load too. Several sacks of provisions, corn, kasava, luggage and people. One pregnant woman was close to term. One boy 'John' I wanted to take the 70-80km to 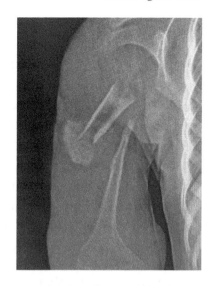 Chitokoloki from his remote village with what appeared to me to be complex osteomyelitis. He was about 5 although no one was terribly sure and he had an open wound with what looked like dead bone sticking through. He seemed to have a non union of a fracture in his upper humerus but in fact it was probably just the result of bony infection. His family unwrapped his dressing - a home made stinking village dressing, at the roadside. The cloth dressing was dropped on the ground and a dog seemed to regard it as a source of tasty nutrition. I was nearly gagging at the smell, the flies and that daft dog! It was a scabby, mangy beast and I can only imagine that it would surely have developed indigestion as a result. Anyway young John was safely delivered to the ward for some blood tests, X-rays, antibiotics and nourishment. I hoped something could be done to help him.

We left at 8am and returned to Chit at 5pm - Dorothy talked the whole time. A legendary performance. I feel like there should be a tee shirt with a logo- 'I survived a day with Sista Dorothy!'

Market!

A quiet Saturday; what a welcome change. I tried to sort out a few problems in the hospital this morning but in the process I made one elementary error which caused a patient extreme pain. It was entirely my fault. The cast of characters involved me and Willie - the man from two days ago with the nasty wound in the most private of parts. He came round to the theatre for a dressing change. In the absence of a nurse I volunteered to deal with him. His wound looked better already. The dressing typically involved using some appropriate antiseptic to clean the area. I am used to using povidine iodine solution which in the UK is typically presented in an aqueous (water based) solution. The African equivalent was sterner stuff and was an alcohol based solution. Well, when I unwittingly applied a liberal splash of the highly irritant alcohol he nearly took off! He let out a yelp and gave a pretty good impression of wingless flight. The reaction only lasted about 10 seconds. Ten seconds neither of us will forget for a long time - especially him. He had a good laugh about it afterwards, was very gracious and thankful and proceeded to do another impression of John Wayne as he walked slowly and carefully back to the ward.

Jenni was keen to entertain some friends this evening. The plan was to make some more flapjacks. The last attempt was a genuine burnt offering. The oven has no temperature gauge or setting so cooking involves complete guesswork. She tried again and made some very good flapjacks this time. Actually she was keen to bake a cake. There was, however, no sign of flour anywhere. I decided to visit the local market. Well, that was an experience. Calling the few ragged stalls and stores a market rather overstates the reality. There was the blue shop. Coke, crisps, sugar, a few biscuits - no flour. 'Where can I buy some flour?' 'The market' replied the nice lady. So I wandered a further half-mile to the so-called market and tried about 4 stalls. Some had baking soda as well as second hand shoes, some had colourful clothes and some bottles of dodgy looking stuff that had the appearance of second hand cooking oil. Alas, no flour. One young man told me that the store across the road sold flour so off I went. It was shut. I asked around - 'Will it open again today?' No one knew. The man with the key had gone! One of the other stall holders yelled at a young teenage boy who disappeared off to find someone to help. Meanwhile, this chindeli (white person) stood around looking at nothing in particular in the hope that the shop owner could be found. Amazingly, a lady appeared, opened the shop and sold me 2kg flour for 20 kwacha about £1.00 so off I went and Jenni rustled up some very nice coffee sponge cupcakes for our guests.

Church tomorrow and two talks to give via a translator. I must remember to be careful about the choice of phrases and culturally irrelevant illustrations.

Reinforcements arrive!

I almost slept in for church but managed to arrive on time - just as they were singing the first hymn. Gordon had asked me to speak twice today - once for Bible teaching and once for a gospel message. My friend Chambula translated into Lunda for me. I took the opportunity of telling the people, who all know him well, how he has many talents and positive characteristics. However, he has one significant weakness - pause for effect - he spends far too much devotional energy following the fortunes of Manchester United. The people all laughed hard and applauded the jibe.

After church, the plane arrived and we went to the airstrip to meet the Kerrigans from Washington State and a maintenance guy called Aaron from Northern Ireland who had been here before with

Brass Tacks[7]. We all went to lunch together and there were many stories to tell. The Kerrigans came during my last trip here in 2015 so it was good to see them again.

I spent the rest of the day reading and relaxing. A FaceTime call home while Jenni slept and I was interrogated by my grandson Jaz who insisted on seeing all the houses. I am not sure he was satisfied with the result. It was difficult to explain anything to him as the questions were coming too fast.

Unscheduled care

We spent the morning wandering around the wards seeing all the patients en masse so that everyone on the team was familiar with what was going on. Doing a head count it is sobering to realise that having been here for only two weeks, at least two of the patients I have operated on have died. In total about 6 or 7 have died but these two surgical deaths were especially disappointing. Perhaps we should not be too surprised as the surgery was performed as a last ditch effort in both cases. Both patients were very high risk. Both were frail with virtually no reserves. Both had advanced disease. It is still disappointing to lose people after investing much effort and hope in trying to help them pull through.

Today, Dr Joel Nkonde from Loloma Mission Hospital arrived with 4 patients. Three are for elective surgery - 2 major cases and one small case. Joel is very popular with the mission staff and seems like a very nice and caring man.

The fourth patient he brought was a poor 17-year-old boy. This lad had endured a typhoid bowel perforation about 17 days ago. He took village medicine for several days and ended up in hospital where Joel operated on him to repair a perforation in his distal small bowel. He did well for about 5 days and then developed peritonitis and an entero-cutaneous fistula. Without further emergency surgery that is a death sentence here. I suggested that he bring him to Chit and he looked pretty septic with peritonitis and dehydration when he arrived. We started resuscitating him and trying to optimise his condition using our best guesswork while Kevin operated on a 5-month-old baby with a bowel obstruction. I eventually gave him a hand and it looked like this child has Hirschsprung's disease. We did a colostomy at the transition point and took some appropriate biopsies. The wee one faces a tough road ahead. That done, we fetched the young man and re-opened his belly. It became clear that the initial repair had broken down and a further perforation was also evident. The most appropriate plan was to bring the offending loop of gut to the surface, convert him to an ileostomy which Joel can close in a few months if he survives. We hoped for a good outcome here but fully aware of the risk that he might become another 'statistic.'

Today, Jenni tapped a chest for fluid, sorted out a sick baby, sutured a gash in the leg of a wee lad who had being playing with knives with his friends. Meanwhile, the two older lads got down to playing with knives as well - just that the game was different.

Jenni had baled out at around 6pm. She came back to the house and became extremely popular when we discovered that she had rustled up dinner for five. So together we entertained Mwansa and the Kerrigans for chicken broccoli bake and salad. Good job Jen! She also made a banana loaf for tea break the following day. What a star!

We are set up to run two operating rooms tomorrow and we have the kit to do the first ever totally video-laparoscopic case in Chitokoloki. All being well, history will be made. Unfortunately, Dr McAdam is not here to participate.

Defeat from the jaws of victory

Our really sick boy with peritonitis looked a bit better today although he is still in a bit of trouble. Getting meaningful information out of patients here is challenge. We had to have a tutorial last night from Mwansa. We have been confused by the reaction of some of the patients. First, not many of them smile. You don't tend to get much of a rapport except with a few. Small children are receptive but the adults generally don't have any interest in engaging in banter. Loads of barefoot kids accost us as we walk along. They always ask: "Ow are yoooou?" a question they will repeat six or seven times irrespective of the answer. When you turn the tables on them and ask the same question - either they will run away giggling that a chindeli has spoken to them or they will admit to being "very fine, please!" One such young fellow was greeted by Jenni with: "How are you?" He replied: "I am fine, how are you Sir?" Hard to know how to respond!

Some of the complaints people have are easy to understand if a little non-specific - "I am paining." Even I get that picture. However when you ask someone how they are, a common answer seems to be: "I am a bit" – that's it. Not a bit better, or a bit worse, or a bit worried. Just 'a bit.' Jenni and I have been wondering what to make of this. Mwansa assured us that it nearly always means a bit better. Only, "nearly always." I am none the wiser!

Another stock phrase response comes when someone is asked, 'Where are you from?' "I am from across." Across? Across what? Usually it means across the river. But whether it is just across or across and continue for 200 km is never clear. Or, I am from "that side" - which usually has nothing to do with being across anywhere. Scotland could be that side and Chitokoloki - this side. I give up!

Anyhow, the big case went well this morning. Then we had scheduled a laparoscopic gall bladder. A first for Chitokoloki! In fact

according to Dr Nkonde, he reckons that perhaps only one other hospital in Zambia has attempted any laparoscopic operations. Our kit all seemed to be working. We got the patient off to sleep and hooked up all the gear on the stack. Insufflator, check. Camera connected, no problem. Light source, ideal. We got the ports in. A diseased gall bladder was identified with lots of adhesions and chronic inflammation. An excellent and suitable case. We started the dissection with a really high quality view on the video screen and mobilised the key structures ready for clipping and dividing. Two clips on - now we were motoring. Then, suddenly a reminder that in Africa things have a sobering tendency to go wrong. Just as I was about to cut through an important structure the video image suddenly disappeared. Huh? A totally black screen. No chance of seeing or doing anything safely. We figured out that the light source had overheated and switched itself off. We let it cool and tried again. Ah, success! We started again. Only 10 seconds of operating this time until – total loss of image. So we managed to find another light source. The intensity of the light was so poor that you could just about make out the structures with the camera positioned impossibly close to them. Not a safe way to operate. We stumbled along with inadequate light and an almost completed operation. The maintenance guys came and struggled to get light from one of three boxes. One was just not up to the mark. One was reliable but the light intensity was not good enough to be safe. One was good but unreliable. In the end, with the operation just about finished, I baled out and made a mini laparotomy to assess the situation and complete the procedure. I was just not confident that we had a good enough view to be sure that all was well. On opening the patient up the gall bladder was safely disconnected and was literally hanging on by the tiniest of connections. Hence defeat from the jaws of victory! At least the staff now know how to set up. They should be able to do diagnostic laparoscopy, perhaps appendicectomy and with a little help, more advanced procedures too. There is a learning curve and a start has been made.

Between the Kerrigans and the Galloways we cleared the queue and only three minor cases remain un-operated. We will get to them on Thursday. Tomorrow the queue will no doubt be reinforced by cases from the legendary outpatient line.

Poor Jack

Picture the scene. One clinic room. It has a couch, a desk, a slit lamp, a dental chair and an ultrasound machine. Add four doctors, two nurses and a succession of patients. Typically there are four or five patients in the room (smaller than the size of an average living room) at any one time. One maybe having a tooth pulled. One having an abdominal ultrasound. One having eyes examined. Another giving a history. Add some children and relatives and stir in some general confusion for good measure. What we need is someone to help us make some sense of the stories the patients tell. They generally answer questions to please the doctor. We must avoid leading questions but without leading questions you get nowhere. Oh - and one minor detail - not one of us has any real proficiency in the local language so we need Jack. Jack is on a basic wage but he works his socks off. He was trying to translate for four of us this morning. Holding four conversations in different parts of the room at the same time. Half way through a conversation with one patient you would hear: "Jack, help!" And Jack would disappear to translate for someone else. Then you would have to call him back to explain to the patient what was to happen next and so on.

'So where is your pain.' "Oh, it's my legs and back and both hands and left ear! And I have paining in my eyes." Kevin and I decided that these patients were only allowed to complain of one symptom.

When you manage to focus on the one symptom it shortens the consultation but doesn't help you get any closer to a diagnosis! "Is your pain worse before food? "Yes." "After food?" "Yes." "Does eating make it worse?" "Yes." "If you don't eat, is it worse?" "Yes." "JACK! Help."

My most puzzling patient of the morning was complaining of bugs **inside** her head! So off came the grubby woolly hat. Time for a careful scalp inspection with gloves on. No sign of any livestock! No, the bugs are inside her head. I can't think of an operation for that particular problem so managed to dispatch the patient to the pharmacy window for some paracetamol. Hopefully that will cure it!

It was Election Day the following day in Zambia. Like elections elsewhere this year it seems like there is not a great choice. The character who is currently in power is unlikely to win the election but it seems he is likely to rig the result to stay in power. So trouble is anticipated. We'll see! I think our translator Jack would make a better fist of it!

Clearing the decks

Jenni and I decided to make a particular effort to go to the staff devotions this morning. We have been there every Tuesday and Thursday, turning up at 7:30am. It was only this week that I learned that they start at 7:15am! That explains why we nearly always missed the great African singing. The hospital staff attend in an outdoor area behind the hospital and typically after three or four songs from the local vernacular hymn book - all sung in harmony, at high volume and with great gusto - there is usually a short message from Gordon Hanna. Gordon is a Canadian missionary. He basically runs the mission station, looks after the maintenance crews, supplies, containers, staff - both hospital and maintenance, -

oversees all the transport, the external links with other groups and coordinates the various visitors. Chitokoloki gets a lot of visitors. Anyway, as the singing progressed this morning – there was no sign of Gordon. I was tipped the wink to stand in for him. I was totally unprepared and had no notice. However, since today was election day I constructed a talk on the hoof and built in a reading from Galatians 5. They were a very appreciative audience. The whole thing lasted about half an hour but, with all the singing, my contribution was only about 5-7 minutes.

We had a quick tour of the wards, arranged discharge for enough patients to create space for today's surgical activity and then went off to theatre. We fixed a couple of fractures, did a hysterectomy, a couple of minor urological operations and an exploratory laparotomy. After lunch the line of patients was getting smaller and smaller and there was a sense of maybe being able to clear the decks completely. Poor Kevin was left with the most technically challenging of cases - a chap with a urethral stricture consequent upon previous sexually transmitted infection. A procedure was required to open up the urinary channel to the outside world. It usually involves passing progressively larger and larger, angled stainless steel curved rods up through the channel to the bladder. If your eyes are not watering by now, they probably should be. This proved to be almost impossible. Various tactics were employed to overcome the difficulty. As I left the theatre they were calling for a coat hanger! I thought it inappropriate to stick around to see what on earth they were going to do with the coat hanger.

The next day was our last full day here. I was coming back to a busy week in Glasgow and then planned to head off for a few days to Kuala Lumpur later in the week. We were both keen to have a compete change of scene and dreamed of a few days on Arran. That won't happen for at least a couple of months. It is always good to get a change of scene and a chance to chill, sometimes literally, in Whiting Bay!

No pain relief!

African patients are tougher and braver than any I have ever come across around the world. If you are fortunate and if the nurses remember or can be bothered and if you have had a major enough operation, you might get a painkilling injection. In Scotland we are so wimpish that following major operations we expect patients to be on heavy-duty pain killers for several days. Here? Three doses would be the maximum!

You need to hear the story of Isaac. He was a bit of a drinker and had a minor operation under ketamine analgesia. Ketamine works a treat and you can do all sorts of surgery, even major cases, with a shot of this incredible agent. Under its influence the patients appear to be 'spaced-out' for a while. As it wears off, they come to their senses knowing nothing about what has happened. However, if the patient is rather too familiar with the consumption of hydroxylated hydrocarbons, a euphemism for alcohol, sometimes in the form of the local hooch, the effects are somewhat less predictable. Isaac was jumping off the bed about five minutes **before** the operation was completed. I was trying to stitch him up and he was fighting with me, climbing off the bed and looking like he was having some kind of nightmare. Three people in theatre, including Jenni were doing their best to keep him under control. One, our friendly nurse, called Womba, was getting nowhere. Suddenly she baled out, with this all out fight in full swing. "I will find Mr. Kayombo!" Mr. Kayombo is big. I was pretty sure that if Kayombo sat on the patient he was unlikely to put up too much more of a fight. Wrong. He just seemed to gain superhuman strength. We ended up with two passing maintenance guys jumping on him as well, and finally I got the last stitch tied and the dressing on as they took him singing and yelling at the top of his voice, down the corridor past all the patients waiting their turn to come in. Not exactly the best psychological preparation.... Note to self – always establish the alcohol history before relying on ketamine alone to keep someone from wriggling. The following morning Isaac was careful to deny any over indulgence. He had no recollection of the events of the previous morning, which was just as well!

It seems that in the aftermath of the elections, there were not so many patients at the clinic today. At the start there were only about six. After two hours' work there still seemed to be about six. Finally, we managed to deal with them all before lunch. It allowed us a leisurely afternoon after another very pleasant visit with the Speichingers. I was able to catch up with some email and organise activities for my forthcoming visit to Kuala Lumpur. Our fridge has been cleared out into our next door neighbour's fridge. Lesley Kerrigan has promised to make us pancakes for breakfast before we fly out to Lusaka. The time has gone quickly but we both feel that the visit has been worthwhile. We have made a definite contribution, it seems to have been appreciated and we have once again learned a lot. Along the way, some good entertainment, some good laughs, some new friends and plenty of stories.

Pancake Addendum
By far the most civilised breakfast we ever experienced in Chitokoloki was enjoyed at 7:30 this morning. Lesley Kerrigan made us pancakes with maple syrup before we set off on our flight to Lusaka. We tried not to appear to be too eager in accepting this kind invitation but it was surely too good to pass up. At 8:15 Gordon came for us in the truck and carted our cases (my minuscule one

and Jenni's enormous one) to the airstrip. There were some locals there to wave us farewell. Some of the missionary staff also came out. J-R and Kaitlin sent apologies because they were in the throes of resuscitating a neonate. Chris always makes a point of praying about the trip before firing up the engine. So with Jenni nervously riding shotgun we took off and made good time to Lusaka. We treated Chris to lunch in the 'Clay Oven' and carried out a couple of errands - we were left with some car parts and a computer which would be picked up by two different people who had been given our descriptions. We hung about the airport concourse and sure enough a couple of people arrived to collect the packages left in our care.

So, what to do? A trip into Lusaka to look around. Perhaps not - the election results have not yet been announced and there was an expectation of trouble. Apparently some of the President's supporters have already been arrested for rigging the ballot count. So we resolved to relax at our guest house until we can check our bags in.

It was too hot to walk around outside and there was nothing to see anyway. It was time to head back to a different civilisation.

Jenni's Chit Chat

Episode 1

It had been just over a year since I last visited Chitokoloki, and I had managed to amalgamate my annual leave between two jobs in order to return for 3 weeks with Dad to lend a hand and get more experience now as a doctor (as opposed to as a student).

I was really excited to return and see the familiar friendly faces of both staff and patients. It was during my first trip to Chitokoloki that I became increasingly uncomfortable with lots of people referring to me as "Doc" when I was in fact - still a student. Chilanda (one of the hard working theatre assistants) was insistent on calling me this even when I tried to explain to him that I didn't quite deserve that title yet. His response was - "Doctor - even when a snake is a very small snake - it can still bite you! So it is still a snake!"

I was very keen to see what changes had occurred (if any) and if I would be of any more use than at my last visit - when I had to hand pick patients from the never-ending queue looking for "easy" cases that I could handle on my own. I was also looking forward to having Dad with me for advice and to show me some surgical skills. Hopefully these updates will provide you with some insight into day to day life in Chitokoloki Mission Hospital from the perspective of a junior doctor who didn't have much experience in working in a rural context.

Here is an update from the first few days.

We arrived in Zambia just over 24 hours ago and already I have seen and heard more crazy things than I have in the last 14 months since I left. I have also succumbed to 3 mosquito bites already! We flew into Lusaka on Sunday and spent the day meeting with some other missionaries who were either coming or going from town.

My favourites so far are Betty and Marion who are 2 missionary ladies in their 70s. They are both half of my height and probably less than half of my weight! It feels very comical to be sitting in between them in the back of the truck!

Betty is a midwife in Dipalata Mission Hospital and Marion is still working as a midwife in Loloma Mission Hospital - despite now being in her 75th year. They are hardy and both wear huge aviator sunglasses that on top of their aeroplane headphones made them look quite the picture. Today, we went around Lusaka shopping for things to bring back to Chit. We drove around in Chris' dilapidated truck but managed to survive. Every time there was a bang or a wallop he would just say "Don't worry we are selling it soon." Ha ha!

So we ended up getting held up in Lusaka for a number of different reasons as often happens in Africa (life here is lived at a laid back pace) and our plan was to fly from Lusaka to Loloma to drop off Marion and then go on to Dipalata to drop off Betty and then get to Chit. Unfortunately, the sun was going to set well before our estimated arrival time at Chitokoloki so we decided to stay the night in Loloma to travel the following day. A blessing in disguise! So I am writing this from Marion's spare room in Loloma! It's been quite an experience already!

We were greeted by half the village at the airstrip and we then headed off to have a tour of the hospital by the local GP and only doctor in the village. He is a Congolese doctor and told me he is not a surgeon but I then found that he manages all the surgical, medical and maternity patients by himself and I also saw him suturing in the middle of the night (more about that later). I told him that after all I think he is not only a general practitioner but a general surgeon and infectious diseases consultant too! The patients had all kinds of diseases including malaria, meningococcal meningitis, active leprosy, fractures, unknown abdominal masses and hydroceles to name but a few. The most awful I saw was a man who had a bad burn injury, probably in his 30s. His whole lower abdomen, pelvis, groin and legs were burned down to the muscle. His right leg was under a blanket but when the doctor took it off the smell was horrendous. His foot was completely black. It honestly looked like charcoal. The gangrene hadn't spread yet but he did look very dehydrated and in a lot of pain. Almost impossible to deal with here with no hope for skin grafting and a shortage of painkillers! It felt a bit hopeless to leave him on a mattress on the ground with no IV fluids but I've since been told that burns often heal quite well without any intervention so we can hope for the best.

We had a lovely dinner afterwards at the home of one of the missionary families. They did a fantastic job of hosting despite that their warning of our arrival was in the time it took for us to fly overhead and land on the airstrip. (More about flying later.)

Jenni and Betty flying first class

After supper, I was getting ready in my room for the next day - laying clothes out and so on and I found a spider on my bed beside my suitcase!! Awful! I couldn't complain or even run for help from the 2 stoic old ladies in the same house. The shame of making a tiny 75-year-old kill a spider the size of a 10p outweighed my fear of dealing with it myself so I put a blanket on it and hoped for the best! Then just as I was brushing my teeth I heard a knock at the door. Rebekah, who is one of the nurses, had come and said: "I've just had a text from the doctor. We are having an outbreak of cow horn attacks at Loloma Mission Hospital! This is the second scrotal injury due to a cow horn in 1 week." She wondered if I would like to come and see! It felt rude to say: "No!", so we drove up in her truck to take a look! The injury actually didn't look too bad though I'm sure was very painful for the patient! He needed about 10-12 stitches in the "crown jewels," as my brother-in-law would say. Ultimately no harm done!

On return to the house there is a MASSIVE spider on the floor blocking my way from door to room! I mean this is the size of two 50p pieces stuck together! Thankfully it's a flat one so I know that they are quite safe and tend not to run. Had to take my chances and bolt past it turning back to make sure it hadn't followed!

I then got back to the safety of my room and found a spider in my bed!! Thankfully, this one, was much smaller. I tried to shake it onto floor and unfortunately lost sight of it! So now I have climbed into bed with mosquito net tucked in, praying this spider is indeed on the outside. Even as I write this, I am feeling tickles on my legs and pulling back the sheets as fast as possible to see if it's there! Dread to think what I would do if I do find it on the inside!!

Going to try and sleep because I have to be up at 6.30am even with the threat of being called in overnight if "anything interesting happens."

No doubt more to follow!

So, today is Wednesday - we have been in Chitokoloki just over a day. The flight here was terrifying for both Dad and me in different ways.

STORY 1 - Terrifying for me, fun for Dad.

So as we were flying from Loloma to Dipalata, Chris (pilot) and Dad were discussing the fact that Dad used to have a pilots' licence. I could listen to the conversation through headphones but could not join in as my microphone had broken - a difficult situation for me as I usually like to have my opinion heard!

So Dad was saying: "Oh yes, I passed the test only 10 years ago or so though I admittedly have forgotten most of it" - in my head I'm thinking, Dad learned to fly when I was about 7 so that's a lot more than 10 years ago! Chris then offered the controls for Dad to take over! I felt the need to explain that 1) I felt Dad had quite misrepresented himself to Chris who was then throwing our lives into his hands and 2) I would feel much more comfortable if our lives were in the hands of the currently qualified pilot instead of the unqualified for more than 15 years "pilot." It's hard to express all of these emotions at once though when you are holding onto your seatbelt and concentrating for dear life on not screaming as his steering was sending us right, left, up and down and all over the place in 3 dimensions.

The plane has 4 seats and responds a lot to any wind, heat, cloud etc. Basically it's quite a bumpy journey for even the less faint-hearted among us. We were also 10,000 feet in the air so I knew if something went wrong we had a long way to fall! My fear heightened as it became apparent that Chris was enjoying the role of teacher and had forgotten how uncomfortable I was about being in the air! He didn't take over again until Dad had almost landed the plane! Imagine looking over the ridge of a rollercoaster at its very highest point before it does a loop-the-loop. Except take away all the stability of the rails - it was like that. I mean looking over his shoulder and then turning the plane a sharp right and down at the same time. I eventually gave up my back-seat silence and tapped dad on the shoulder and firmly pointed that Chris should now be in charge. I think he was quite relieved for a way out without giving up his aura of courage!

STORY 2 - Terrifying for Dad, fun for me.

On flying from Dipalata to Chitokoloki, Chris decided to take the scenic route "flying low" over the flat terrain. He took us right down and basically followed the river all the way back to Chitokoloki. It was amazing; we were just at tree level and felt almost like skimming the water. We could see people waving along the road and even went directly over man on a wee boat who probably thought we might decapitate him! The views were incredible and I felt very fortunate to get such an experience! Following the river required quite sharp turning that added to the excitement. Dad was trying to hide his concern ... "So are there any low wires in this area", "Oh wow, I didn't expect this thrill ride!" He later explained that flying low is more dangerous as you have no time to manoeuvre the plane before crashing should something go wrong. My thought was - sudden death, sudden glory! Better than a long fall!

The hospital is as crazy as ever. Over the last day I've seen more burns patients and they are really gruesome to see. They are apparently more common at this time of year as everyone sits round a fire at night. It's winter here though I would hardly have noticed. One girl had burns on her arms up to her elbows from putting her hands into a vat of hot porridge! Dr. McAdam had to examine an 8-year-old boy today with facial burns to try and find his eyes behind all the swelling. That was one of the worst things I've ever seen...though, thankfully, his eyes were healthy looking.

Dad and I did a hysterectomy on a woman with cervical cancer. We tackled the clinic queue with patients with all sorts of ailments ranging from itchy scalps to pus coming from the eyes, from neck swellings to pregnant mothers with no foetal movements. I still find myself perusing the patients' notes along the queue until I find one I think I'll be able to deal with and discharge without guessing what I'm seeing on an ultrasound and leave the hard things like swollen abdomens or eye injuries to Dad and Dr Mwansa! Theatre work can be hard as the lights tend to go out for short periods and we have to wait for the generator to start up. When we first arrived there was no water! It is difficult to scrub for an operation in such circumstances and hard to shake the feeling that you are a walking carrier of disease!

Things I enjoy about being back

- Seeing patients that I met last time and noticing they are better!
- Meeting with the other staff here - everyone is so friendly and welcoming and glad to have our help - I don't know if they realise how out of my depth I am!!
- Bright orange sunsets
- Incredible views of the stars
- Brightly coloured outfits everywhere you look
- Effortless singing in harmony
- Hilarious stories about close shaves with snakes, crocs, angry mobs and other adventures!

Hopefully I'll be able to send a less rambling and more concise report next time with some patient stories and more about my escapades as I try to be an anaesthetist! So far I managed to anaesthetise a child quite well for the duration of his short operation but forgot to take a note of any of the observations the whole way through! All praise for my anaesthetic skill was revoked when this was noticed!

Have to go - can't complain - Dad is making my dinner!

Episode 2

The female ward is full just now and I had to take a picture of the patient in the last bed who is receiving a blood transfusion whilst lying on the floor! So here we are - portraying the image that we are using our time, skills and training to help at the mission hospital and serve patients in some way or another. I find myself sorely lacking in usefulness in all walks of life here and am almost definitely more of a hindrance than a help!

I have greatly appreciated all the replies to my emailed report. It is good to have the encouragement. Maybe these anecdotes of my failings so far will give you a little perspective into the limits of my abilities!

My further attempts to become an anaesthetist have failed miserably. I have had one more opportunity to do a spinal anaesthetic in a man who needed an emergency operation for a strangulated hernia (basically a loop of bowel had become stuck through a weakened part of his abdominal wall and the blood supply had been cut off and the bowel was dead). I saw my chance to do a spinal anaesthetic and set about to carry out the procedure with much enthusiasm! Got the patient ready, picked my spot, cleaned the area, inserted the needle hit some bone, readjusted, hit more bone, readjusted again, finally got into the space between the bones! Feeling quite happy with myself, I removed the inner part of the needle to see if I had got into the right space. If I had, crystal clear fluid would be running out of my needle indicating I was in the spinal canal. To my horror, fresh blood seemed to be pouring from my needle! Dad reassured me that eventually the blood would clear and sure enough, clear(ish) fluid started draining so I quickly attached my syringe and pumped in 3.9ml of anaesthetic as fast as I could to produce the desired effect. It's meant to make the patient unable to feel anything from about the belly button downwards and be unable to move his legs.

Well?

My poor patient gave quite a yelp as Dad made the first incision in his belly indicating that perhaps my spinal hadn't quite done the job. We waited a while to see if it would eventually kick in. Still quite a response to pain, this time legs kicking to go along with the squealing and grimacing. By this point Dad and I were both scrubbed and ready to operate but the patient was still awake and moving! This was a kind of an awkward situation when the anaesthetist was to blame but the anaesthetist is actually yourself.

We finally gave up waiting and hoping that the spinal would work and did the operation with ketamine - a drug rarely used in the UK but essential here as patients go to sleep but continue to breathe! A rare benefit as anaesthetic agents go.

When the patient woke up at the end and was still kicking his legs, Dad was kind enough to suggest that perhaps the spinal had worn off. I'm not sure it ever wore on! Who knows where I put the 3.9ml of bupivicaine! No patients were ultimately harmed in this procedure but in fact, a life saved thanks to dad and absolutely no thanks to me.

The other slight problem in this case was that I had been quite tired all day. I was blaming the heat of the sun and the jet lag along with arriving straight after an on-call block of days and nights and being exhausted. I was feeling very sorry for myself so I had a long nap (rarely available in Chitokoloki) and woke up to go back to hospital to help in this case. After my failed spinal and getting gowned and gloved I began to feel quite hot and queasy. Along with the queasiness, as Dad began to open the abdomen I also could feel my vision slightly closing in from the outside. Difficult to decide what to do in such a situation as I am sterile so if I give up it's a bit of a waste of precious sterile gowns and gloves (which are in short supply). But when the big lump of dead bowel came squelching through the abdomen and Dad started burning the arteries to stop them bleeding, I quickly admitted defeat and went and sat in the corner.

Not only a failed anaesthetist but a failed surgeon too! All good lessons to learn - maybe the Lord wants me to be a geriatrician after all?

My other failure in the last couple of days has been in an attempt to keep up good 'brethren' hospitality. It was Saturday today so I had the afternoon off and we had a whole chicken to roast so we invited a few missionaries round to our house for dinner. Thankfully, the main meal worked out well but I decided to try and bake a cake. All the ingredients were in supply except for the flour! Thankfully, I found a lemon drizzle cake mix. Who knows what I did wrong but the cake had a huge crater or two in the middle and was very very dark on the bottom of both sponges! I was quite horrified when I saw it come out of the oven and even more horrified with each attempt to hide the mess under icing. It ended up looking like a child had attempted to make a cake and I was in the unfortunate position to have to serve it to people whose, baking skills are far far superior. Dad, who is usually quite encouraging of my baking attempts, even had to laugh out loud when he saw it.

Thankfully, the guests we had were kind and said it tasted ok!

Sad moments

Some more interesting patients this week...

There was a patient in ICU named Charity who was a bit of a mystery. She was admitted with very low conscious level and was very distended with fluid build up in arms, legs, abdomen and even her face was puffy. She didn't have a surgical problem so with 2 surgeons running the ward round I decided to try and investigate the lady to the best of my ability. Maybe she had kidney failure? Kidney function had been normal a week before and while she was making urine there was no way to repeat a creatinine level as the man in the lab has gone; who knows where! No one is going to Zambezi today. Sometimes, there is a possibility to run extra tests there but it is more than an hour's drive away. Maybe this was liver failure? I scanned the liver, couldn't find anything specific to treat. Today, while I was doing the ward round by myself I noticed her heart rate was 160 beats per minute - the fastest I've felt so far I think and she was also unresponsive, even to pain. I asked whether it would be possible to get a full blood count (simple lab test) and a chest x-ray. Oh well, the man in the lab was still gone and the radiographer lived very far away. So we added some antibiotics and other medications, about the limit of treatment we had available. It is almost impossible to know exactly what to do when you don't know what you are treating! Our most likely diagnosis was that maybe she had taken some poison that her body was responding to as she had a big distended bowel. However, she did have a fever so we thought it could have been an infective cause. Lab tests were eventually done which confirmed our diagnosis of sepsis. It was unfortunately too late and we heard that, despite treatment, Charity passed away that evening.

There was a child who always seemed to have a ready smile but unfortunately he only has one hand now as he needed amputation because of the damage produced by a snake-bite.

There is an 8-month-old baby whose mother is "reactive" that is she is HIV positive and she had not been compliant with treatment throughout her pregnancy and even while breastfeeding. In fact, she had been feeding the new born with nshima! So the baby was very unwell and likely to die of the complications of HIV when already at risk due to malnutrition. It will be a completely unnecessary death which simple health education and good care could prevent. We are doing what we can with build up drinks and antibiotic treatment along with HIV medication, but the result is not likely to be good.

There is a poor young man who had been in a road traffic accident and had a fracture of both the tibia and fibula of his left leg. He had gone to some dodgy hospital in Angola where a rogue doctor of some kind or another had put what looked like a thick metal rod into the bone to try and fix the fracture and then held it in place with a short length of twisted metal wire. It looked like the wire you would use to close a sandwich bag. An absolutely terrible job of trying to fix a leg and an x-ray like I haven't seen before. Unsurprisingly, the patient was having problems with pain and so had decided to come to Chitokoloki for a second opinion.

On the road (quite a long and bumpy one), part of this wire that had been put into this leg actually ended up popping out through the skin! I don't know if any of you have had a fracture repair but I hope you would be as shocked as I was about an internal fixation ending up as an external fixation! The poor patient was in a lot of pain but thankfully Dr Georgio (quite a charismatic Italian surgeon) was here and took out all the metalwork and did his best to do a proper repair. Unfortunately, he isn't sure whether it is too late for this leg and the patient might need an amputation when he comes back to review.

Good moments
- The orthopaedic team have come and measured up around 30 patients for prosthetic limbs - a lot more people are amputees here including young folk as their conditions don't present to hospital until it is often too late to save the limb.

- A young 8 year old boy on the paediatric ward seems to have paralysis of his lower half, perhaps as the result of an accident in the past. He is always so cheery on the ward but undergoes a lot of suffering every day. He can't move and has acquired huge infected pressure sores on his bottom and his back. They must be very painful. Dr Georgio decided his best treatment would be in a specialised spinal unit in Lusaka. The logistics of getting a paralysed boy from a village with his mother and baby sister to Lusaka for a prolonged hospital stay seemed insurmountable. However, as it happened, Chris was flying to Lusaka the day after his review with an empty plane! So we got things organised in remarkable time (for Zambia) and I watched the 3 of them fly off to Lusaka today for proper specialised care. Quite amazing that this is possible for him and that his care will be free as the hospital is a charity. Chris said when he first turned round to see his reaction to the plane he was holding on to the ceiling and walls for dear life! But after a couple of hours he was sleeping with his arms behind his head quite relaxed and accustomed to this new experience.

- Relaxing and reading books today in the sun with a relative lack of big bugs
- Hot water in our house while the rest of the mission seem not to have any :)
- Good conversations and time spent with friends J-R, Chris and Christina tonight at our house - hearing more ridiculous stories and catching up!
- Getting email replies from around the world!
- I don't think my emails are long because they have a lot of content, I think they are long due to much rambling on my part - for that I am sorry.

I'm going to bed now because it's 0030 and my contact lenses are making my eyelids stick down and we have church at 0900 ("it won't be this in the morning"). Also there is something hitting our tin roof and I feel much safer under my mosquito net...

Eh mwani, Jenni

Episode 3

One of the orthopaedic patients who has been on traction for months has now had her operation and is mobilising around the hospital with an even bigger smile than usual! No one could find the supply of ultrasound scanning jelly - it was being used to provide weight for the traction system designed to hold her bone in place. No wonder we couldn't find it for ages!

Monday

Farmer's day! Zambians love a public holiday and so do I! The ward rounds were completed in the morning. I love the atmosphere of community here in the hospital. Community essentially means absolutely no privacy. If you ask a patient a leading question such as: "Have you been doing your exercises?" or: "Do you drink much alcohol?" the patient will always respond and tell you the answer you want to hear. The give-away sign is that the rest of the twenty patients in the ward all crack up laughing when they hear the lies! Indicating to you that things may not be as they seem! As we traipse from bed to bed down the long line of patients and then back up the other side, everyone's ears and eyes are on the patient in question. Not only other patients but their caregivers too who might be any family member from grand-son to great auntie and their dependants along with them and, of course, any "blue man" (a cleaner) who may be passing by and helpfully edge into the conversation to translate! Everyone gives their tuppence worth whether it is required or not. The heckling makes me feel quite at home!

After the ward rounds, we fixed a couple of fractures. Dad decided this would be good experience for me. We looked at 2 x-rays, one of a little girl with a broken leg and another a teenage boy with a fractured arm that was slightly out of place. Mwansa and I had to pull the arm back into position while the boy was asleep! As it turns out she is much stronger than me! I got to put the plaster on both the patients. Apparently, there is even a wrong way to put a bandage on... I am learning fast!

The rest of the day felt like a real holiday! We had lunch at Sista Dorothy's (one of the missionaries and a real character) and then Mwansa (the other doctor) and I fancied a game of ping pong. We spent the afternoon on our friend's verandah playing, chatting and drinking coke out of a glass bottle (life in Africa at its finest!). The afternoon was long, restful and enjoyable. It ended with a surge of adrenaline though. Mwansa wanted me to drive her quad bike back to my place. Easier said than done. It's a big bulky machine and the go pedal is actually a handle at your thumb and the gear box is actually a pedal you kick (why would you mix these two essential driving tools up?) We both nearly hurtled off the back of the truck when I changed from first to second gear - much to our amusement!

Tuesday

The second of August was a great day to be born! I always say that it is always sunny on the second of August and unsurprisingly this year was no exception! The day started with loud rousing Lunda hymns in staff devotions sung in perfect harmony! We then went to theatre. The first case was a Caesarian section that turned out trickier than we first thought. Dad was operating and I was assisting though the nurses liked to comment that by the way I was talking it seemed I must have done more of them than he had! "Are you sure you want to do that?" or "I'm not convinced that's the best position to be in" and so on. I can't help but keep Dad on his toes. It makes me feel better to know that he is sure of his position at all times.

This was this lady's fourth Caesarian section and she had placenta praevia. That meant the abdomen was going to be a bit more hostile than normal with lots of previous scarring. I've always known that sections can bleed a lot (because there is increased blood flow to the uterus so the whole organ has a very rich blood supply) but I've never seen so much bleeding up close. As soon as we got into the abdomen and started getting through the muscle layers of the uterus there was a torrential outpouring of blood from all over the place. I was panicking and sweating and Dad was desperately trying to clamp as many bleeding vessels as he could. It seemed to me that he was clamping lots of small bleeding vessels when the main torrent of blood was coming from a different place all together. I liked to helpfully remind him: "She's still bleeding", "Dad – there's more blood, we haven't got the main bleeder yet", "The swabs are soaked Dad - there's still a big vessel we haven't got yet." Poor Dad was very patient... "Yes, Jenni, I can see there is still bleeding - it's hard to think about anything else!"

Eventually, we made the decision to get the baby out as fast as we could and try and stem the flow of blood once the risk of suturing the baby's head was out of the way! Out came a beautiful wee crumpled baby girl! The rest of the operation was significantly bloody but much more successful and the sight of J-R the multi-tasking, multi-talented nurse-midwife who was taking care of the anaesthetic carrying the newborn around in a wee sling was cheering to even the most stressed surgical assistant! The poor lady needed a unit of blood but actually still had a reasonable haemoglobin by Zambian standards (7g/dL) despite the whole ordeal.

It felt like a very apt way to start my birthday by holding my new birthday twin! I went to check on the Mummy later and the family informed me they wanted me to name the baby! I was a bit overwhelmed with pressure as I was the first time I was asked to name a baby. I suggested 'Joy'. As it turned out the Granny is called Joy! So I said what about 'Skye' or a Scottish word like 'Bonny'! They

Jenni and Bonny

opted for 'Bonny', which made me laugh. The wee bonny baby is doing very well and will probably go home this week.

After the section, we had a second party to celebrate my birthday! J-R had made an amazing birthday cake for me, which we had at tea break. The whole surgical team came in and I even had candles to blow out! The rest of the day we spent operating and then in the evening played games together with some other hospital staff and missionaries. A great day!

Wednesday

A normal day, providing one is comfortable to be flexible with the concept of normality. All systems go! Mwansa, Dad and I, all seeing patients at the one time and Jack our translator hopping between us all!

Thursday

I do not know how this happened but I ended up on the ward round by myself. Dad said a quick hello to those in "intensive care" and then toddled off to theatre and everyone else disappeared. I quite enjoy the banter on the ward round and making my own decisions! In this hospital I find myself discharging patients, stopping antibiotics (people seem to be on cloxacillin for months at a time and in my opinion that's asking for antibiotic resistance!), increasing pain killers (maybe I'm too soft) and for any that are too hard to deal with I say, "You go to theatre and ask to see Dr Galloway senior!"

A new patient had been admitted with a leg wound. None of the nursing staff were enthusiastic about undoing his dirty bandage so I told myself: "Don't be proud Jenni - this is a job for you!" You can imagine my horror as a large pus-filled wound was exposed which was absolutely CRAWLING with MAGGOTS. I could not have retreated from that bedside any faster! Maybe not a job for me after all! The smell was awful. These weren't nice little sterile maggots like you get in Britain to help wounds heal. These were massive fat yellow flesh-eating maggots that were falling out onto the bed and the floor. I immediately regretted my choice of flip flops that day! Still itching at the memory.

On the round I noticed a very sick baby whose mother had HIV and for some reason none of the medication that she had been prescribed had been given! She was severely dehydrated and had thrush in her mouth. At only 8 months old she looked like a new-born and was only 2kg in weight. I picked her up and she was completely floppy and didn't even have the energy to cry; worrying for a baby! Most scream at the site of my chindeli (white person) face! I took her along to theatre so Dad and Mwansa could assess her and help me put an intravenous line in. I honestly thought she might die in my arms as I walked along the corridor. My instinct wasn't to look at her just in case she did - I would have been so horrified. Isn't that weird that my instinct was to run away? I had felt the same during the blood-spilling-everywhere-Caesarian-section but didn't have the choice.

Anyway, we managed to get a cannula in and gave some fluid. Dr. Mwansa put a tube into the stomach and I gave 3 different nurses a severe talking to, to make sure she got the prescribed feeds and medication. She began to look a bit perkier by the end of the day. She survived the week and I was left hoping she would do well although she remains very sick so, at best, a guarded prognosis.

On my ward round I also met a new patient who spoke English and said: "Doctor, please look at my problem" which turned out to be his penis! In these moments I have to remember my profession and not say "No thank you very much!" Gathering my courage I did look and could not believe what I saw. This man had a large wound on his penis such that I could see the urethra inside it! The skin had all rotted away. It was absolutely terrible. I said, "This man needs to be seen by Dr. Galloway senior" and passed the burden to Dad. He was also shocked and got some of the other nurses to come and have a look. It turned out the patient had married a woman in Angola from a different tribe and required a circumcision 8 months previously. Because of untreated HIV infection his wound hadn't healed and the tissue had broken down. Awful. He might even need an amputation! Horror of horrors.

Dad has started referring to him as Willy. Terrible, but strangely funny at the same time.

Thursday

Tonight we were going to have people round for games so I made flapjacks but then a couple of people cancelled due to feeling tired or having other commitments. So we texted everyone to say: "Come tomorrow instead." Good job!! The remains of the "flapjacks" are flaked into a bowl for Dad to have for breakfast tomorrow. My baking attempt was absolutely abysmal. Our oven (always blame your tools) seems to burn things on the bottom and not thoroughly cook on the top! Nightmare. Used up my only cake ingredients and now when people come round tomorrow we have genuinely nothing to give them. Not even a biscuit!

Friday

More ward rounds and clinics for us. One of the more interesting stories concerns another patient from Angola who sustained a gunshot wound to the eye during the civil war and has been blind in that eye for the last 20 years or so. Then last July, while out chopping wood, a piece flew up and hit his good eye, instantly blinding him. He has spent months trying to get transport to a hospital to no avail. Last week he decided with his wife to walk to Chitokoloki - a journey that took them 7 days. The wife led him by the hand the whole way. There is probably very little that can be done for this eye as the injury occurred about a year ago and he has had no vision since. He has some response to light. I had the unhappy job to explain that he would probably not see again. He suggested maybe an eye transplant? It's difficult to explain the impossibility of this helping his vision. What a shame.

There are LOADS of malnourished babies, eye infections, hernias, hydroceles, and those with rectal bleeding here. Schistosomiasis is prevalent and lots of people have chronic symptoms of liver disease with varices which can cause catastrophic bleeding. An unpleasant condition for patient and doctor alike. Patrick, who is the child with facial burns that I previously mentioned, has done surprisingly well. The swelling in his eyes has gone down so he can now see again and the wounds are doing well. Burns treatment here is incredibly different from the way it works at home, but the results seem good nonetheless.

Saturday
Little doing - lots of reading and baking and relaxing!

You will be happy to hear that my attempts in anaesthetics and in the kitchen have improved slightly! Have done 3 successful spinal anaesthetics since I last wrote and I've made as many edible cakes now as I have burnt! So those are better odds. And I've also done a couple of operations by myself albeit with someone close at hand.

One of my solo operations was for a poor wee boy with a big abscess under his chin which I had to drain. Should maybe have taken my sunglasses off before I started!

I had the opportunity to close an abdomen after a major operation. This is meant to be the easy bit! My problem was that I developed a sore back because the operating table here slowly sinks down during the operations! It can be elevated by pumping a foot-pedal but it slowly and imperceptibly sinks down again so, before you know it, you're bent in the middle deep in concentration trying to fiddle about with tiny instruments and needles! It's honestly so difficult. Dad sutures big wounds in no time and I fiddle around for ages just

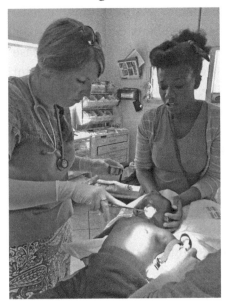

trying to get my needle on the needle holder (which to me looks just like just about every other instrument on the tray!) Mwansa was also saying that I kept putting the needle in too deep. She wanted me to go along the line of wound just under the surface of the skin. If I dared venture into subcutaneous tissue she would say: "Too big!" We are talking in millimetres! Absolutely no mercy for my shaky hands and achy back.

In other news -

Did you see a Boeing 777 crash landed in Dubai airport this week? An Emirates flight. Guess what type of plane and with what airline and to which airport we are going next week! Dad says this happening definitely reduces the risk of it happening to us! That has not done anything to calm my nerves though.

We are looking forward to our last week here. You never know what's going to happen next. It's very entertaining watching Dad try and fend for himself in the kitchen. All the confidence he has at the operating table has gone! Also looking forward to being home and drinking real milk and washing my hands and not be horrified by the brown water that washes away.

From your favourite Zambian chindeli
Jenni

Western concern for global surgery

From December 2015 – December 2018, it was my privilege to serve as President of the Royal College of Physicians and Surgeons of Glasgow. The College is an ancient institution providing education and assessment for doctors in hospital practice in the UK and beyond. It was originally founded in Glasgow in 1599 by a Scottish surgeon, Maister Peter Lowe, who had spent much of his career on the continent serving as a military surgeon in France, Flanders and elsewhere. After the siege of Paris in 1589-90, he described himself as being 'Chirurgian ordinary to Henry the fourth, the most Christian King of France and Navarre.' When he returned to Glasgow in 1598 he was horrified at the standards of medical and surgical practice in Scotland and successfully sought and obtained a Royal Charter from James VI in 1599 to establish the institution that has now become the Royal College. His concern was the development and maintenance of high standards of care. With many rogues and charlatans around, not to mention trained physicians and surgeons who had a tendency to, over-charge and exploit the vulnerable, the College used its statutory authority to examine and license practitioners – particularly surgeons in those early days. The College continues to have an international role in the preservation of high standards and best practice in clinical care. Interestingly, following the death of his first wife Lowe married Helen Weems (or Wemyss) who was the daughter of Rev. David

Weems the first Protestant minister of Glasgow Cathedral at that time. Lowe died in 1612 or 1613 and is buried in a well-preserved and rather impressive tomb against the south wall of the Cathedral churchyard.

During my term of office, I was very keen to make a coherent response to the desperate international need flagged up by the Lancet Commission report (see page 22). A young Christian colleague, Stuart Fergusson, took a year aside from his clinical training in general surgery and joined the College as a full time Fellow in the Scottish Clinical Leadership Programme. Stuart's desire was to raise the profile of international volunteering by staff in the Scottish NHS and to provide a clear-sighted report for the Scottish government that would demonstrate the mutual benefits of the formation of successful partnerships, both long-term and short-term, between health service employees in the UK and hospitals or health systems in need of sustainable development. Stuart (who has also spent some time in Chitokoloki) was instrumental in influencing the Scottish government with the production of his report; *Global Citizenship in the Scottish Health Service*.[8] This work had generated a great deal of interest within the College community and around the Scottish NHS and it became increasingly clear how much interest there was in the opportunities to build sustainable partnerships. While my duties made it difficult to spend much time in Africa, I was keen to return especially because I knew Chitokoloki would be without their surgeon; David McAdam was traveling to Canada for his son's wedding.

Some of my reports from previous visits had 'leaked' beyond my family and friends and people were keen to receive regular updates from the next adventure in Zambia so I styled the following section initially as a blog for the College readership. It was circulated widely and for the purposes of this volume I have edited it to preserve the flow and sense of what went on during the summer of 2017.

President's Blog: Zambia

I travelled on a Malawian Airlines flight from Lilongwe to Lusaka before connecting on to Chitokoloki with two colleagues, Chris and Canadian trainee nurse, Hannah. There was good chat all the way on the Cessna 206, 9J-CTO, and on landing we were met by Julie-Rachel, whose roles had extended even further! Apart from all the non-hospital work she does, she functions as a hospital manager, surgical registrar, consultant anaesthetist and club foot expert. Dorothy, Kaitlin, wee Owen and members of the maintenance team were also there to welcome us. I had just missed David McAdam, normally the sole doctor here as he had left that morning by road for Lusaka.

Pulling my bag off the plane, J-R announced they were expecting an ambulance from Lukulo with a patient who had a suspected splenic rupture. He had been beaten up and was thought to be bleeding internally. He was whisked into theatre while I grabbed something to eat and then went to assess him. He seemed pretty stable with a reasonable blood pressure and while he had a racing pulse and was dry, we gave him a fluid challenge. He responded quite well and so parameters were agreed such that if his pulse or blood pressure breached limits in either direction I should be called. He remained stable all night so it was a good decision not to rush in to operate!

"I am paining doctor!"

Monday started at 7:30am with a long ward round that involved seeing everyone in the hospital. There were, as usual, lots of patients with uncertain diagnoses. A group were invited to 'Sista' Dorothy's for one of her unusual lunches. Apart from the odd wee potato-like roots which tasted of liquorice – the rest of it was very appetising. There was a monster clinic in the afternoon and I did not even try to count the patients in the seemingly endless queue. Towards the end – there were all sorts of people with little wrong. Failing eyesight. Painful joints, in one case the history went back for several years. I got to the stage of using my usual trick of allowing the patients the chance to complain of only one thing. "I am paining doctor!" If the initial presenting complaint turned out to need no real intervention there were always many other symptoms in the wings – totally unrelated to the first complaint, which were then brought into play. It is almost impossible to make progress with cases like this! I felt the need to develop a different tactic when, as a final straw, the last patient complained of being dull of hearing in one ear. I was close to the end of the rope after many hours in the consulting room and apart from the other pressures the Clinical Officer's handwriting was so bad – he or she might as well not have bothered writing anything. It transpired that this patient had had his hearing problem for 15 years! I reassured him and encouraged him out of the clinic so fast that he must have wondered what just happened! We worked on until 18:15 then went to theatre. J-R had been struggling to deliver a stillborn baby with a face presentation. She eventually had to reposition the baby into a breech position – unfortunately the whole process had appeared to shred the cervix. I made a repair and returned the patient to the ward.

I had listed about a dozen patients for surgery so we had enough work to be going on with. Dr Joel Nkonde, our friend from Loloma, sent on some x-rays for a 20 year old lad with gastric outlet obstruction. He clearly needed surgery so they intended to set off with the patient the following morning at 5:00am to get him here so that I could operate on him. There is also a 16-year-old girl in the ward with pelvic inflammatory disease and a big bilateral tender mass in her pelvis – likely a tubo-ovarian abscess. The main differential would be a complicated ectopic pregnancy but her pregnancy test was negative so she was prepared for laparotomy the following day. In the UK she would have IV antibiotics, a couple of dozen blood tests and a CT scan. She would then likely have a radiological drain placed. None of that is possible here – the only solution is to take a knife to her and make a good sized opening, confirm the diagnosis and sort it out. If we continued to accumulate cases at this rate, I feared there would be no chance of getting them all done.

When I finished, I went to Joey and Kaitlin's for a meal and finally got back to the house at about 20:30. I then prepared a teaching session on acute abdominal pain for Wednesday morning and collapsed into bed at 23:45.

A chance to cut – is a chance to cure!

This aphorism, the origin of which is not clear, is oft quoted by surgeons. I headed up to theatre and had a quick look in the ITU before getting busy. I ended up operating on a total of 10 patients today. Dr Nkonde's gastric outlet obstruction boy turned out to have peptic ulcer disease with pyloric stenosis so we did a laparotomy and a Roux-En-Y gastro-jejunostomy. This is an operation that removes part of the stomach and creatively re-routes the intestinal channel in such a way that it functions well while avoiding some of the problems of re-joining things in a somewhat more straightforward fashion. Medical students tend to have difficulty in understanding the concept but it works really well and to the patients' benefit. I took Joel through the case so he could hopefully tackle this kind of thing in Loloma in the future. The other timeless principle comes into play here - 'See one, do one and teach one' – only compressed a tad! I then did a couple of hernias, a hydrocele, scoped a patient who turned out to have gastric cancer and will need a distal gastrectomy and reconstruction later in the week. I also dealt with some minor gynaecology in the form of a cervical polyp, banded some varices, faced an awkward umbilical hernia which had me sweating a bit when some troublesome and unexpected bleeding enforced an enlargement of the incision to sort it out, and did the laparotomy on the young girl with what turned out to be a bilateral tubo-ovarian abscess. The small bowel was plastered to this and it was a little difficult. Tragically in this society her problem is the result of teenage promiscuity, which is rife here. She ended up with horrendous pelvic infection and will most likely be sterile. That too, is difficult to bear in this culture.

One highlight of the day was a video call to my dad in Scotland, right from the operating theatre. He follows the missionary news updates from Echoes International and had read about the work here and about some of the staff so he was intrigued to be introduced to J-R over the internet and have a conversation with her.

Axes, bullets, a single kwacha and a croc hunt

Happily, all of yesterday's patients seem to be in good shape. Some are a tad grumpy but since the only meaningful post-operative pain relief is paracetamol I think they can be forgiven. I started today with a teaching session on acute abdominal pain. There was a good attendance from nurses and clinical officers. I had been warned that the attendees don't like being picked on to answer questions in an interactive teaching session. So I forewarned the clinical officers yesterday that they had better be ready. When they all filed into the classroom it was interesting to see how people (the world over, it seems), headed for the back row! So just as I started the session I announced that I would only pick on people in the back row. Rapt attention! Good engagement also.

Later, whilst on the wards I was in my comfort zone until we got to the maternity section. I was only asked about three difficult obstetric questions and, of course, I knew the answer to none of them. How on earth do I know what to do when a mother starts to bleed four days post delivery? At least the girl was warm and well perfused and looked good from the end of the bed. She even smiled at me. A smile is a very important and reassuring physical sign. Rarely do shocked patients or people with peritonitis or major bleeding manage to manufacture a smile.

Before getting to the 20 or so clinic patients, I was summoned to theatre because a young guy had been chopping something with a large axe. He missed his target but connected with the medial aspect of his left ankle. There was blood everywhere! I arranged an x-ray before attempting to explore the wound or sort things out and sure enough he had a compound fracture and had chopped right into the medial malleolus – the lower part of his tibia at the ankle. This was quite an accomplishment with a filthy and rather blunt axe. The wound itself bled but more from the fracture site than the soft tissue so I put him back together and left the question of what to do with the bone for a visiting orthopaedic team who were due to arrive the following week. I reckon it will be fine as there was minimal displacement. After he hopped out, I saw another chap, Patrick. He had been shot up and ended up with bullets in his abdomen and in his left hip. His left leg had been so wrecked that it had been amputated above the knee before I got here. Now he has an established vesico-intestinal fistula – an abnormal connection between bowel and bladder. He was keen for something to be done for that. I tried to get a cystogram which involves putting contrast material, which shows up on x-ray, into the bladder so that a road map can be created and thus allow a reconstruction to be planned. Unfortunately, he also now has a urethral stricture so I could not get access to his bladder – more action for tomorrow under ketamine! My old boss used to say that there was no point in doing easy cases. Maybe!

The monster clinic failed to materialise so I went walkabout with my camera and planned to get some shots in the village and surroundings. I came upon an intense football match next to the airstrip. The local team (Chit City) was playing their rivals (Young Stars) and they were whipped 3-0. It looked like most of the village were there to cheer them on – quite the community affair.

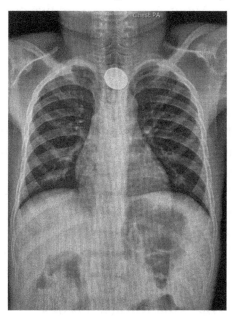

Wandering back I was accosted by a local. "Doc – Sista J-R is looking for you at the hospital." The bush telegraph – literally. The problem was a wee lad of seven who had swallowed a single Kwacha coin and it lodged in his upper oesophagus. X-ray confirmed the position and we anaesthetised him and set about trying to retrieve it with a combination of a rigid scope and a pair of alligator biopsy forceps. This is a potentially risky business – I never did really learn the art of rigid oesophagoscopy. I was able to grab it, just and no more, but did not get enough of a grip to extract it. Plan B was to slide in a flexible endoscope and gently push it on into the stomach. Success! A single kwacha is worth 4p!

Making my way home after this, I was invited to go on a croc hunt in the River Zambezi. I was too wary the last time I was here but felt that I couldn't chicken out this time! So what's involved? Well the whole exercise is best accomplished under the cover of darkness. You have probably appreciated enough from what you have read here already to understand that the river is not the safest of places. The plan was to get in a tiny boat, in pitch darkness, start up the outboard and navigate our way out into the current. The view of the night sky was truly spectacular with an amazingly clear view of the Milky Way. There were five of us aboard. One, Chris the pilot, driving at the rear, one, Joey the maintenance wizard, up front with the searchlight, one (me) with the rifle and two spotters who were both bulky Irish visitors. You need to understand that with such a crew the diminutive craft felt far from stable. The moon had gone by about 10pm and we covered about 5-6 km hunting for the light reflex from crocodile eyes close to the banks for some 90 minutes. No joy. I was glad I borrowed an extra fleece because it was really cold out on the river. A similar crew had been successful in killing and retrieving a 10 foot croc a couple of days before but given the risk of being dumped in the river especially if there was any attempt to pull a half dead beast out of the water into such a precariously balanced boat, I was secretly praying that no crocodiles would come to harm that evening. Mercifully, that prayer was answered.

"What kind witchcraft is this?"

Today felt like an operating day in the NHS – just in a totally different environment. At home the operating rooms are spacious and full of shiny high tech kit. I am used to cupboards being tidy and organised. It is usually easy to find things. Everything is properly classified and in the right place. Most items are single use. Here, the working environment is a total jumble. Things are a much more cramped. Much of the equipment here is second hand and a good deal of it doesn't work or doesn't work as expected. Only one person (J-R) has a fighting chance of finding an obscure instrument or drug and you just have to hope that she is around. Nothing, not even single use items are considered to be 'single use.' All the disposable items including anything which is not stained or contaminated – indeed almost everything is recycled or re-assigned to a different role. Items which are used (but clean) such as disposable surgeons gowns are chopped up and used to wrap instruments for autoclaving. Single use surgical staplers are cleaned and submerged in antiseptic rather than being lobbed straight in the bin!

For the major cases today a newly trained clinical officer assisted me. He was getting the hang of things and I tried to encourage him and show him a few tricks as we went along. We did a challenging distal gastrectomy for a newly diagnosed gastric cancer, a paediatric hydrocele, a urethral stricture, an abdominal rectopexy and a couple of other unmentionable cases that I should really not describe here for fear of producing psychological morbidity. The stomach case was excellent – we had to take our time around the pancreatic head because of lymphatic extension of the tumour and it all went really well. The rectal case was a bit of a 'dig' under spinal anaesthesia and with only modest muscle relaxation, it became something of a fight the whole way.

Anyway, in a break between cases, I decided to put in a few family internet video calls. The only person I could reach was Jenni who was travelling in Edinburgh in a friend's car. I let her speak to Kayumbo the senior theatre technician because, of course, she knew him from her two previous visits here. He was totally astonished and could hardly put a coherent sentence together, being so amazed at the reality of a video call. "Can she see me?" he kept saying. "Oh no Doc! What kind of witchcraft is this?" That had to be the quote of the day. He was then connected to another previous visitor in Northern Ireland by J-R who was also in theatre. Again – lost for words! Best entertainment I have had for a while! Oh, and the kwacha emerged – found you know where, by the patient's granny!

"How are you?" "Doc, I am a little bit fine"
There is a crazy cockerel close to the house I have been given. It has no sense of propriety. It starts crowing anywhere from 2:30am till 5:00am. As ever, the day starts in the hospital at 7:30am. We assemble and start in the ICU before heading into the seemingly chaotic wards. Some patients speak English and that makes it easy. Some speak a kind of English such that in response to: 'How are you today?" "Fine," I think 'usually' means 'OK' whereas "a little bit fine" can mean that 'I am feeling pretty dodgy!' I spent most of the morning fending off patients with guessed diagnoses. It is about as much as you can do when the only readily available test result is a haemoglobin level. On some days of the week we might get a creatinine level although not usually on the days it might really be required. Radiology in its simplest form is available and a portable ultrasound machine is also available – the issue is that you not only have to perform the ultrasound investigation yourself but also try and make sense of the images. A challenge! I even read a 12-lead ECG today – not bad for a surgeon. Normally I would be pleased if I managed to hold it the right way up!

I had to think hard about my urology training. A middle-aged man pitched up with a tight urethral stricture. It is possible to stretch the narrowed passage by carefully navigating a series of graduated bougies of increasing size and weight through the external plumbing system and round the various corners into the bladder. (Men may wish to skip the rest of this paragraph!) The instruments are kind of J shaped and getting into the bladder with a series of rigid stainless steel instruments is not pleasant for the patient or the surgeon. However, a bit like riding a bike, I managed to negotiate the terrain. I felt chuffed that the task was accomplished without too much in the way of patient protest! I did require a shower soon after the procedure though as I was unable to dodge some of the airborne fluid. Enough said!

I got through the clinical work and after lunch (which is the main meal of the day here) dealt with some email and wandered off to the river. It is a very impressive and beautiful river. It is just such a shame that it is teeming with nasty wildlife like crocodiles, schistosomes and tiger fish. Four wee girls approached me and walked with me for a while, announcing that they wanted to be my friend and to come to my home in Scotland. They were wearing filthy rags and know nothing of the outside world beyond their patch of the bush. Despite being 10 years old and attending school the oldest of the four, Happy, was unable to read. The others were Theresa, Precious and Joyce. Joyce was four years old and wandering around being supervised by these other scalliwags!

I am hoping the hospital remains quiet as I am essentially on call 24/7 for the next 16 days! I have also been asked to contribute by speaking at the church service on Sunday morning. I need to give that some thought and be careful to strip out any culturally irrelevant phrases or ideas. I think it might be best to steer clear of any humour. The Glasgow variety just does not seem to hit the spot here.

It's a bugs life
After a quick tour of the hospital and a minor procedure I spent the rest of the morning preparing what I am going to say in the church service tomorrow.

Seeing the pattern of morbidity here makes you realise that while there are risks from the wildlife we generally associate with Zambia, much of the morbidity results from tiny beasts of one version or another. According to the WHO, the most significant bug in terms of purveying misery and death is the mosquito. These in turn carry all sorts of really nasty pathogens. The second biggest killer is schistosomiasis or bilharzia (named after Theodor Bilharz; a German physician and surgeon who described the offending trematode in 1851). For you classical scholars, the word schistosoma means 'split body' which is because of the shape of the male beast. This area is awash with both mosquitoes which carry malaria and the fresh water snail hosts which are essential to the life cycle of the schistosomes. A double hit. The mini bugs are certainly holding sway here.

I got off lightly because there was no emergency action in the hospital. One admission caused concern as a possible ectopic pregnancy. Happily she settled and I have stayed out of the way.

Colony death and bush funeral

I managed to give my wee talk in the church via an interpreter – my friend Chambula Chimwanga. He is such an enthusiastic leader and determined to share the gospel with his community.

I had been invited to attend a funeral for a poor lady who was well known to most of the mission staff. Being curious as to how this would all play out, I went along. The lady who died had lived with her husband in the leper colony near the hospital. She was about 80, had bad asthma and had weathered several critical complications in the past. This time she unfortunately died before reaching help.

The leper colony consists of four rows of tiny single room houses. They are the size of a small garden shed but far less well appointed than any sheds I have ever seen. There must be about 60 of these buildings. They have no furniture. They are really just a shelter and that is about it. Just as in the 'Old Hospital' I have already described, here also the cooking is done outside over an open fire. There is, of course, no water and no power. They are grubby and some are falling apart. There are not many actual lepers left now but this lady's husband is one of the remaining leprosy patients. She was his carer. He is both blind and unable to walk. He has no fingers on either hand so you can imagine how difficult life is even although he is mentally alert and articulate.

The funeral was a real eye opener. About three hundred villagers gathered in a big church building. There was loud hymn singing followed by even louder wailing and screeching which reached an almost hysterical level when the simple coffin was carried in. After about an hour, everyone set off to walk to the 'cemetery.' This involved a trek across sandy soil around the airstrip through some very primitive villages to a completely undeveloped area of bush. I followed the crowds and came to a clearing where a deep grave had been prepared in the sand. I think this is the northern edge of the Kalahari hence the nature of the ground. Everyone gathered around and again there was much wailing. The coffin was brought along a nearby track in a Toyota pickup by one of the Canadian missionaries and several of the hospital staff man-handled the coffin to the edge of the grave. There were no ropes or cords in sight so I did wonder how this was all going to work.

I was not quite prepared for what happened next. Suddenly two young men jumped down into the grave. I was standing nearby but when they jumped in they completely disappeared from sight! It must have been at least 7 feet deep. They then received the coffin, which had to be tipped up to about 60 degrees off the horizontal, and gently lowered in. I could not see quite how they proceeded although one climbed out leaving the other guy to position the coffin before climbing on top of it and himself being helped out. It failed to have quite the reserved decorum sometimes completed with top hat and tails that we are used to seeing in Britain. There was some praying then preaching and then a team of four fit chaps with shovels started filling the grave in while everyone stood around. There was a flurry of activity with dust flying around and the hole was filled in within about 4 minutes – certainly no more! Everyone was then presented with a twig from a bush – we were really trampling on bushes as it was a completely unprepared area. All these twigs were subsequently gathered and were placed in a little trench which was prepared in the top of the mound of sand covering the grave. Then about 15 or 16 women knelt down and sang beside the mound and smoothed the sand off with their bare hands. The whole event was really very moving. After that, the elderly leprous widower was carried to the graveside by one of the Canadian missionaries and he spoke in a strong voice – in Lunda so I could not understand, but he spoke about his deceased wife. How he will get on now – I dread to think. There is no welfare state here!

Where is the justice?

There was a real commotion outside the hospital entrance this morning. "It's a thief!" was the announcement. A chap had been captured in the act of pinching a blanket from an attendee at the wake which followed yesterday's funeral and not only was he not quick enough to escape, it turned out he was the prime suspect for a number of other thefts which had taken place recently. I could not resist the temptation to go and have a look. Here was the prisoner wriggling and protesting, hog tied with ropes around his hands, tied behind his back, and his feet tied together. Apparently the police had been summoned to come and take him away but since they had no fuel that was not an option. Community justice took over! He was being huckled into a car and hauled off to be beaten up, or worse. There must be a good chance that, should he survive, he will be back in the hospital before the close of play. The prediction is that he is likely to get less of a beating from the family of the victim than from the police so maybe he is better off where his is. Bush justice in action!

Today is a public holiday in Zambia. The Chitokoloki football field is the location for a knockout competition featuring 8 teams from the region. Quarter-finals today and semi's then the final tomorrow. Enthusiastic, sometimes skilful players, who have to contend with a surface that is more suitable for beach volleyball, hotly contest these matches at high intensity. The crowds have been large and vocal. It is a real community event. The ball squirts and bounces in all sorts of unpredictable directions so the goalkeepers face particular challenges and some have been humiliated several times today.

I was about to give up being a spectator and get out of the sun when the 'bush' telegraph located me – "You are wanted at the hospital." I guess I am conspicuous – the only white man and the only person with white hair in a crowd of 500 spectators. When I arrived in the paediatric intensive care area the team were trying to resuscitate a 3-month-old baby. He was a twin. He had also been operated on for Hirschrung's Disease which is a congenital bowel problem and having developed problems a few days before he had become progressively worse. His poor parents who were so caring and attentive to both babies were distraught at the turn of events. When I saw the child, his heart had virtually stopped and he was having CPR. He was already tubed and ventilated. His blood sugar was OK, he had already had four doses of adrenaline and it was clear that he was about to succumb. I heard the father ask: "Is this the end of my son?" as he was given the pathetic little bundle to hold for one last time.

Tragically, he was only one of two baby deaths that day. The other little one was only 6 weeks old. He was contending with an omphalocoele, which is the result of imperfect fusion of the anterior abdominal wall. The paediatric team in Lusaka had agreed to take the patient when he reached 9 months of age. There was virtually no chance of surviving 9 months in conditions here and while we do not know what the mechanism of death was – probably sepsis – I fear that this baby had virtually no chance.

Strangely enough, these contrasting accounts in one day call the seeming injustice of suffering to mind. At least the parents of these babies will have some support from the Christian community in the Mission Hospital – a feature that is not so easy to come by in the modern NHS!

Shootout!

Patrick is the young man who, thanks to a shooting, is without a left leg below the upper third of his thigh. He also has the fistula between bowel and bladder or at least between gut and urinary tract. The exact site has been difficult to determine. I had good reason to believe that the problem might be accessible via a surgical approach to his abdomen and pelvis. That was proved to be wrong. I spent a couple of hours following and mobilising his rectum from within his abdominal cavity all the way to the pelvic floor and there was no sign of the suggested fistula track which appeared on the contrast radiology from last week. I then decided to have a look from below and identified a low track connecting the prostatic urethra to the upper rectum. When we then opened up his perineum, it was possible to disconnect the abnormality and reconstruct things. Four hours of surgery but hopefully with a good outcome. After lunch – I did a routine hysterectomy for big bulky fibroids and a few other cases.

So what about the shootout? Well today, half the hospital staff were missing. In reality they were about 300 yards away at the Chitokoloki 'stadium.' Actually it is a nearly flat patch of a very dusty sandy field with imaginary line markings to make it a functional football pitch. The tournament which had been unfolding over the previous two days finally came to a climax as we were finishing in theatre and two local teams were contesting the final. There were officials complete with flags and whistles (liberally blown as appropriate) and there were crowds! Those cheering on their teams numbered at least 1500 at an educated guess. I arrived as the two teams who had managed to see off opponents from other parts of the region were locked at 1-1 with some 5 minutes to play and a sun that was fast sinking on the horizon. There are no floodlights here. Actually to be more specific, there are no lights here! The final whistle was blown and this match was therefore to be decided by a penalty shootout. The crowds surged on to the field and assembled about 8-10 deep in a small area within the imaginary box around one of the goals. The referee paced out the distance and selected the penalty spot and the teams readied themselves. The Young Stars were the competition favourites and had played some good football. They were probably the best-organised team. The opposition was called the Red Arrows – incongruously decked out in bright green. Some of the locals could hardly get over my innocent suggestion that they might be better called the green arrows. Anyway to cut through the atmosphere and the palpable excitement the Arrows scored their first three penalties with consummate skill. The Young Stars managed to hit the post and then had their next two efforts saved by the Arrows keeper. Game over – the favourites had lost the shootout. Great drama.

More teaching and speaking tomorrow and again on Sunday, so headed home to do some preparation.

BID – Brought in Dead (nearly!)

Wednesday was a routine day in the clinic after a well-attended early morning teaching session. There was the usual variety of unpredictable pathology. Even with an interpreter it is virtually impossible to take a meaningful history. The answers which come back generally bear no relationship to the questions which are asked. Eventually, I just gave up. The only excitement was an urgent call to theatre, which also serves as the resuscitation area. A young man was brought in, not breathing, unrecordable blood pressure, virtually no circulation and a desperately low blood sugar. This was an open goal and should have been an easy fix. He was given 60ml of 50% dextrose intravenously and he woke up and was chatting in about 2 minutes. Miraculous! It is quite satisfying when someone is brought in looking almost dead and was then able to walk out shortly thereafter very much alive. He did not get away before hearing one of my sternest lectures about the evils of tobacco and alcohol. It was clear that he was a bit of a chancer. In fact, there is a plentiful subculture of people who had they lived in Glasgow would be regarded 'ne-er do weels' or chancers.

A day of controlled violence

This was probably one of the most intense days of surgical experience that I have ever known. It started simply enough with a laparotomy for reconstruction of a gut in a young woman who had an ileostomy performed after resection for dead bowel back in March. No bother. Then I had two battery acid cases; these were tough. One, a young girl of 16 who swallowed the acid to injure herself in order to make someone, against whom she had a grudge, feel bad for her. The problem is that caustic injuries to the oesophagus are usually devastating and not infrequently they gradually produce a fatal outcome. The gullet narrows down over a short period of time until it closes off altogether. The girl could just about manage to swallow her own saliva but virtually nothing else. She also had a tracheostomy because the damage involved her airway. Her nutrition was by means of a gastrostomy tube. On passing the endoscope from above it was impossible to be sure of the anatomy of the stricture. It was possible to introduce the fibreoptic gastroscope from below via her gastrostomy opening and after much effort I managed to get at the oesophagus from below. It was tricky because of the angle of incidence of the gullet into the upper stomach and it took about an hour of failed attempts until it was finally possible to get at the narrowed section from this approach. I was then able to thread a guide-wire up and ran a series of graduated dilators over the wire to about 1cm diameter. This was a modest improvement and while it was better than a pinhole it was still not very satisfactory. I then threaded a long heavy gauge suture up through the track so that it came out of her mouth at the top and out of the gastrostomy in her abdominal wall. It was then possible to pull some successively larger dilators to get it stretched up to about 1.5cm. Result! She ought to be able to eat reasonably well although will need the process repeated on a regular basis over the next several years. Tragic really.

The next case was similar – only worse. However it was technically easier to achieve more or less the same result by 'railroading' these dilators through the narrowed segment. I was not brave enough to go beyond 20Fr or about 0.8cm for fear of splitting the gullet and ending up with an even more serious problem. We had a few more scope cases, found another gastric cancer, a case of oesophageal candidiasis in an HIV patient and a peptic ulcer. There is plenty of pathology for sure. I was glad when the long day appeared to be over – except it wasn't.

I did manage dinner before having to go back to operate on an emergency. The doctor in Zambezi Hospital sent a 15-year-old lad who had intestinal obstruction and peritonitis. At emergency operation he was found to have a caecal volvulus (a twisted portion of bowel which had compromised blood supply as a result). The damaged bowel was gangrenous and to add insult to injury, there was a perforation to repair. By the time he was sorted out it was 10:30pm. Happily, there were no more cases after that.

A high speed thrill ride

The orthopaedic guys are here today with a monster operating list. Dr Georgio Lastroni is the Italian orthopaedic surgeon I have met a few times before and he was accompanied by Jim Turner. Jim is an Edinburgh graduate who trained in Glasgow and Oxford and decided to take on humanitarian work rather than work in the NHS. He has done fellowships in CURE Malawi and in Toronto's Hospital for Sick Children. CURE is a Christian Mission dedicated to helping children with deformities and they have a chain of hospitals all over Africa.

The two visiting surgeons were very impressed by the Chitokoloki hospitality and the work ethic not to mention the fact that it is mainly funded by churches and individuals in the UK and the US.

One of the particular pleasures of this trip was an introduction to the legendary Dr Ros! She is a paediatric neurologist from near Oxford and comes out to Chitokoloki for three months at a time alternating with three months in the UK where she picks up some locum work. I knew of her reputation but our visits had never coincided before. It is good to have a professional kids' doctor who knows what she is doing! So many of the children have various tropical diseases as well as weird and wonderful things that I am pretty much out of my comfort zone in the paediatric ward. We'll leave it to Ros from now! I was certain I would learn a lot from her.

J-R came looking for me about a patient we had treated the day before and who was in the ICU. My phone was charging and I missed the WhatsApp message. She came hunting for me and came to the door of the house. I was sitting outside, reading a book and enjoying the sun unaware that she was frantically trying to locate me. Eventually I picked up the message and discovered that J-R had been banging on the door of the wrong house! You could hardly script it.

Towards the end of the day, we took a call from a village about a guy who had been badly beaten and was having difficulty breathing. I decided to go out in the ambulance that was driven by Joey Speichinger. The road was a single-track sandy path with high grass and potholes everywhere. We had to take an excursion through a forest to avoid a fallen tree and then speed on; rocking and rolling until we arrived at the village. There was a small crowd around the casualty all peering at the funny white guy with white hair. The patient was badly bruised but didn't have anything critical. It seemed prudent to take him back to the hospital and I figured he'd be a lot more uncomfortable after the ambulance journey. We lifted him and set off. It took about 40 minutes of driving along these ridiculous roads through the bush to get back. We lived to tell the tale and took some video along the way.

I had a good discussion with Jim Turner who, while he acknowledged the value of the Christian principles behind the CURE organisation and the support from churches and Christians around the world, himself has but a nominal interest and no active Christian commitment. He was so impressed with the missionary team here in Chitokoloki – he felt that they have been treated so well, and with extraordinary kindness and hospitality, he said: "This is just like heaven!" A good witness for sure and it is hard to miss the dedication and love shown, by the team here, for the people in their care. It is a privilege to be part of it.

Mufwaha and some late night obstetrics!

A slow day. Saturday started with the nice Italian orthopaedic surgeon wandering into each ward in turn and yelling "Mufwaha" at all the patients. He was merely trying to locate his patients amongst the partially blanketed forms lying in the beds and on the floors – in wards, in corridors and even outside in the courtyard. Puzzled; I asked what this mysterious phrase was. In Lunda it means "Bones!" He was calling for all the Mufwaha patients from the day before so that they could all be seen and examined before the team flew off. Good technique.

I saw the orthopods off the premises and after surveying yesterday's damage, dealt with a totally hysterical woman who seemed as though she was dying of acute abdominal pain. In reality, there was very good evidence that she had absolutely nothing wrong with her. It was a slow day until 22:30! I was called to see a patient who was essentially in obstructed labour. There had already been two attempts to deliver her with the vacuum device, but no success. We thought it best to get this baby out without further delay. Happily it turned out to be a straightforward Caesarian delivery. No anaesthetic just a syringe full of ketamine. The quotation, attributed to the British science fiction author, Arthur C. Clarke: "Any sufficiently advanced technology is indistinguishable from magic"[9] comes to mind here because ketamine would be in that category. Indistinguishable from magic. It was a good call because the baby was becoming increasingly distressed. Dr. Ros who has a neonatal background came along to receive the baby and both mother and baby are now fine after the usual trauma of a long, then obstructed labour followed by a significant emergency abdominal operation.

Flying surgical service

It was Monday morning and I met Mr Kayumbo, Mr Katota, a Clinical Officer, Dr Ros and Chris the pilot at the airstrip. We flew for 15 minutes to the short tree flanked airstrip in Dipalata deep in the bush. We had the first operation done before 9am. That is not commonly achieved in the UK! In fact, latterly it was almost never achieved because of all the built in and totally unnecessary faffing around that now goes on. I met a nice couple from Northern Ireland – Tommy and Margaret Craig, who have been instrumental in building various facilities on the Mission Station – including the hospital, maternity unit, extension, wells, water towers – you name it!

We had our six cases done by lunchtime. They were all minor cases including a bilateral tubal ligation to surgically sterilize a woman who has completed her family. What a fiddle that procedure can be. It would be far easier with a laparoscope – instead it feels like fishing around with a finger trying to locate each Fallopian tube in turn and make sure it is divided and ligated. This woman delivered more than a month before so her uterus was almost back to its normal size. The ovaries were hiding and it took about 10 minutes to secure the first tube. The other one gave up with less of a fight. It seems that vasectomy is not commonly performed here. The men rule the roost. The women carry the heavy loads both literally and figuratively.

Betty Magennis who runs the maternity service here made us the most amazing lunch – a chicken curry followed by an extremely generous helping of apple crumble. I was so glad I had all the cases done by that time. I went to explore the neighbourhood in the afternoon and walked about 3 miles with a farmer who told me about his family and his philosophy of life in excellent English. He wanted to show me his local river, the Lunyiwu, a tributary of the Mekondo, which in turn drains to the Zambezi. I was more than slightly uncomfortable and extremely watchful when I heard all the snake stories he was keen to tell me. He was keen to know about Scotland but has no chance of ever travelling there. He has 5 children, just about manages to subsist, living in a simple typical mud house. He does, however, have a bike that cost him 100 Kwacha at the market. Riding it must be almost impossible because the roads are all deep sand tracks. It is literally like walking along a soft sandy beach. Every step sinks in enough to make it feel difficult to make progress. After I left him I retraced my steps to meet the plane. A young girl caught up with me and tried to keep in step. Local villagers on either side were heckling her and they appeared to be teasing her about walking with the white man and when I picked up the pace she would fall behind and then run to catch up. It was clearly doing something for her street cred and she obviously enjoyed that.

We took off and flew back to Chit at low level i.e. about 1000 feet until the flood plain beside the big river, then at about 25 feet above the surface of the water. I have strict instructions not to post the video on social media. We'll see. Once again I watched a poor man in a dugout canoe duck as we flew overhead at about 25 feet above him. The return journey was a highlight to end the action for the day. Once again we are facing too many cases tomorrow....

The flying patient service

Tuesday was a heavy operating day again - 13 hours, although admittedly one of these was a break for a very nice lunch!

It started off with a man whose name was Fairness. Some of the people have fantastic names. Lots of Bible characters are represented although generally not the ones we encounter in the UK. Names like John, James, David, Esther, Deborah are not so common. Here, however there are plenty of personifications of Job, Moses, Enoch, Ezekiel, Isaiah, Tabitha and many more. Just a sample of the more unusual examples I have come across include Marvellous, Pretty, Happy, Wisdom, Gift, Prince Philip, Socks and even Nobody! I wonder if we should encourage this fashion in the Western world?

There was plenty of banter in theatre today. Some good quality Zambian personal criticism was being traded between the Scottish surgeon and two likely lads, Kayumbo and Katota. These men are great workers but are not averse to displaying the characteristics of a couple of mischievous characters when the circumstances permit. Our patient, poor old Fairness, had a resectable gastric cancer. The staff are getting used to seeing a gastrectomy with a Roux loop reconstruction and they anticipated all the tools we would need which was most impressive. I did some more gullet stretching for the two acid swallowers and managed to stretch them both up so that they will be able to eat a little more than before – something they have been unable to do for many months. I was about to start another case when a plane with Jonathan and Jo Lake (respectively pilot and midwife) from Kalene Mission arrived carrying an Angolan lady who had suffered intestinal obstruction for about a week. She was really unwell and I was wishing for some laboratory support. I had to make do with a potted history and a referral letter which gratifyingly informed us that some unspecified blood tests were normal a week ago! I did not feel reassured by this encouraging but totally useless piece of information. One might even say that it was not exactly relevant to this presentation in a woman who had been vomiting and becoming increasingly dehydrated for days on end. What chance does one have with all the odds stacked against this poor patient? From examination it was clear that she needed emergency surgery. I found a colonic obstruction with a pelvis full of fixed tumour. The only option was to divert her bowel and hope that she will be more comfortable. She is not long for this world I'm afraid.

That took up a good chunk of the afternoon and the queue of patients sitting on the bench outside the theatre were told that their surgery would have to be delayed and that they should return the next day. The response was typically polite, "Eh Mwan" which roughly translated means "Yes please!"

So I only now have three days to tidy up here and hopefully leave everyone appropriately treated. There will be no surgical cover for the ensuing 10 days before Dr Andre Trutter from Canada flies in, a week or so before the resident surgeon, David McAdam returns from the UK. It does leave the staff rather exposed. To be honest I wouldn't fancy being a patient in any African hospital I have seen, let alone in a hospital that couldn't get me out of a surgical pickle if required. Time to appeal to a higher authority!

Just a bit!

All the post-operative contenders from yesterday seem to be in good shape. After the ward round and the essential tea and buns at 10am it was off to the clinic. The queue was as for an execution.

Trying to take any kind of history from a local Zambian patient is, I have reluctantly concluded, a lost cause. It seems that if they can indicate the approximate anatomical area(s) wherein resides the malady – they have done all that is necessary. Attempts to elucidate symptom pattern, associated features, even duration are largely fruitless and totally confused. Symptoms also seem to flit around – oddball pains in the legs, the upper arm and the back of the head and do not infrequently accompany pain and odd feelings in the abdomen. After giving strong reassurance on the basis of the consultation and giving an opinion that nothing serious is wrong and no treatment is required; that is when a new suite of previously unheralded symptoms are then brought to the fore. I have given up and just adopt my veterinary approach. Physical signs I can see or feel – they have a reassuring objectivity. The subjective stuff is just impossible. A steadily increasing proportion of outpatients are now being sent away with the strong message that there is nothing wrong with them. They mostly do have some chronic disease of course, malaria, bilharzia, anaemia and nutritional issues and they clearly have symptoms of some kind – but no signs, so they leave downcast with no new treatment. Frustrating! A case in point – a woman came to the clinic today complaining bitterly of pains in her joints. Which joints? All the joints! No exceptions! All, she said were swollen, she was unable to walk and hardly able to move. Well she moved pretty swiftly to the examination couch. There was no joint swelling visible. Her range of movement was impressive. There were no other discernible features. No fever, no malaria, no sickling.

Zilch. The solution? Well for a diagnosis, I have literally no idea. The treatment – a cinch! "Panadol 2 tabs three times daily and come back in a month if you are no better!"

Amidst the apparent malingerers and complainers there are some really sick people. An elderly man came today – his official year of birth was 1908 making him 109 years old. That seemed unlikely. It is much more probable that something has been lost in translation. He really needed a 60,000 mile service including cataract surgery, prostate surgery and a few other things best left unsaid. I have another woman who has been a diagnostic puzzle for the last two weeks. There are times when she seems fine – eating, drinking, moving around – no fever and here is the key point – nothing objective. Yet she moans and complains and writhes around the bed – mainly when the medical team arrive mind you. On examination she appears to be totally normal. Well today her husband sought me out to show me something she allegedly 'passed.' Passed from which orifice I wanted to know. On examining the said object it was about 3-4 cm across somewhat spherical, black and decidedly unpleasant looking and roughly the shape of an onion! (You do not want to know which orifice but it was one not normally associated with the passage of any kind of solid or semi solid object). I suspect that the witch doctor has been having a poke around and has inserted some village 'medicine.' I am sure she is a NOAP and has Non Organic Abdominal Pain.

I have also given up trying to understand the meaning of the stock response to the question: "How are you today?" The answer invariably is: "Just a bit." I have tried the obvious and logically coherent follow on. "Just a bit, what?" There is no point; "just a bit" is all you are going to get. I even tried a series of leading questions – insert as appropriate; 'just a bit, better? Or worse?' No, none of these. "Just a bit!"

An early start

It is not that hard to describe your emotions when your phone rings at 3:18am and Julie-Rachel proffers a cheery invitation, "Fancy coming to do an early morning section?" It is certainly not a great feeling. I pulled on some clothes and wandered up to the hospital, which was about a 5 minute walk. I did the section and was back in bed by 0430. Result!

I agreed with the rest of the team to a 09:30 kick off rather than a 07:30 start. I managed one hernia case before being summoned to the delivery room where a young woman had become very unwell. She was at about 35 weeks in her second pregnancy and to all intents and purposes looked like she had peritonitis. The baby's heartbeat was not detectable on ultrasound whereas 24 hours before it had been fine. I interrupted the planned operating schedule and took her straight to theatre for laparotomy and Caesarean section. On opening the abdomen – there was a lot of blood – it looked like a major intra-abdominal haemorrhage. At first I wondered if we had twins on board but in fact the baby was lying in the abdominal cavity but outwith the uterus and with its membranes intact. We delivered the still-born baby and puzzled for a few seconds as to what was going on. Then it dawned – the patient had ruptured her uterus. A little more exploration revealed the extent of the problem. The entire front of the lower half of the uterus was wide open, bleeding profusely and so after delivering the placenta, we set about getting control. There was no prospect of putting the uterus back together again so I ended up doing a subtotal hysterectomy. These complicated obstetric cases can be pretty difficult.

To cut a long story short, we completed the rest of the list of 10 minor cases and as I was leaving the hospital I went to see this girl again. She didn't look great and about an hour later I got a call to return as soon as possible because she was clearly bleeding again. All the signs were that we were not able to keep pace with the loss and she was as pale as an African could possibly be. We took her back for another laparotomy – under ketamine again (I think it is my favourite anaesthetic agent), found a modest bleeder in the right adnexa and an abdominal cavity full of blood. The measured drain and surgical loss was some 3.5 litres! She was on the point of arresting when we managed to get some un-cross-matched blood into her. Two of the missionaries with O negative blood came to the hospital and donated 500 mls of fresh blood each and when that was transfused she began to clot again and metaphorically turned the corner. By this time it was about 8pm.

I told Kayumbo he could have the rest of the day off! He giggled at that thought, on and off for the next half hour. Eventually I made it to Joey and Kaitlin's for a cheeseburger, most convivial; sitting around their patio fire under a canopy of magnificent starlight.

What a day! Come back Dr McAdam – all is forgiven!

It's Owen's birthday – Cake Smash

Unfortunately, almost as soon as I walked past the guard at the hospital door I was told of an emergency in the male ward. An elderly man that we have been looking after for the last 3 weeks collapsed. An airway was established and he was whisked quickly out of the ward and along to theatre;

not because he needed surgery, it's just that all the resuscitation equipment, oxygen, and so on is available there. We did make an attempt at CPR but he had fixed dilated pupils and there was no sign of any electrical activity in his heart on ECG. Breaking such news to a family through an interpreter is not the most pleasant way to start the day. I saw about 2 dozen clinic patients and did a couple of minor procedures before heading for the cake smash.

I wrote about Owen last year when he was newly born. His mum had been a 16 year old girl who delivered him in a remote village across the river and about 5 hours away on foot from Chitokoloki. Her wee boy was delivered after a prolonged labour but, unfortunately, she bled. Without any medical help she had little chance of survival and she passed away on an ox cart on the way to hospital. The father, a young destitute boy whose life was focussed on keeping body and soul together by subsisting on whatever he managed to grow, was in no position to feed or look after the baby. So, the young American missionary couple, Joey and Kaitlin, offered to foster this wee fellow. They named him Owen. His natural father was so pleased with this that he was keen that they go ahead and adopt him formally and after a year of due process that has now officially taken place.

Owen is a real wee character. Now standing and staggering around holding on to furniture he is nearly walking without help. Today was his first birthday and part of the celebration involved a cake smash. Now this is a somewhat foreign concept and, having seen it, my view is that it is almost entirely without merit. All the many guests at the afternoon birthday party were offered the kindest of hospitality. All had a mini birthday cake in the form of a very nice homemade cupcake. So far, so good. However, the birthday boy took up position in his high chair and an enormous cake (such as would have fed all the guests with plenty left over for the rest of the week) was placed in front of him. He proceeded, tentatively, at first to dig into the heavily iced sponge with his bare hands. After a few minutes the entire cake was well contaminated by baby slobber so anyone who thought they might be offered a slice had certainly lost any appetite or aspiration to share! Nevertheless, he seemed to enjoy his day and was quickly on a major sugar high!

Being more philosophical; what a transformation in his destiny has taken place as a result of the turn of events. He will now have the opportunity not only of a loving and well equipped home, but an education, proper health care, and real opportunities for the future. If his mother had lived – he may well have had a loving home and a contented life but would likely have been poor, living in squalor and exposed to every disease around here. The legacy would be one of a lifetime of chronic illness, without opportunities for education or to fulfil his potential. A real conundrum.

Heading to the airstrip for 8am tomorrow for the flight to Lusaka where I anticipate the airline, Emirates, will transport me back to a different sort of insanity.

Unable to stay away - 2019

Noise

I had forgotten about the sounds and smells of Lusaka. Arriving into Kenneth Kaunda International Airport I enjoyed the benefit of knowing, at least, a few of the ropes. On a previous occasion I had joined a long slow moving queue to obtain an entry visa. One open desk, a less than enthusiastic employee and a plane load of passengers to process proved not to be a great combination if ever efficiency was considered to be desirable. I am not a huge queue fan especially as a participant. So on this occasion I had the foresight to select a seat near the front of the aircraft and as soon as the doors were opened I set off across the tarmac apron at a march, managing to overtake almost all of the 40 or so passengers who had been in position to disembark before me. It was a case of head down and focus! So I ended up third in the line and was pleased to part with my 50 USD for an entry visa after the shortest of delays.

Got to the CMML Flight House and was aware of the contrast between suburban Lusaka and the village of Whiting Bay on the Isle of Arran where I had spent most of the previous week. Arran is almost completely silent but for the distant crashing of the rather underwhelming surf. In Lusaka there is a veritable cacophony; dogs barking, roosters crowing, music blaring, traffic surging along and people shouting. It is frantic and chaotic in comparison to Hebridean gentleness and peace.

I met Andrew Williamson, a construction specialist from Toronto. He has come to spend the next 5 weeks in Sakeji School in the north of Zambia. We enjoyed a few hours of discussion ranging through politics, theology, economics, science, the history of the Christian brethren movement, LGBTI issues in schools and the social contagion that is transgender ideology. He has a great respect for people like Jordan Peterson, Ben Shapiro and others and is very up to date on the problems and personalities involved in the Brexit issue in the UK. It turns out that he knows several friends of mine from Scotland. Small world!

Chris Brundage, the Chitokoloki Mission Pilot, arrived in Charlie Tango Oscar the Cessna 206 which has had a completely new paint job and looks very smart indeed. I was able to meet Chris' sister Caitlin and her friend Sarah – both Emergency Room nurses from northern Canada and now on their way back home to work.

We made our customary trip to Shoprite to buy provisions, some frozen food and fruit and revisited the Hungry Lion where it took Andrew and me about 5 minutes to figure out how the queueing / serving system (such as it was) actually worked before we were able to order some food. It is rather like McDonald's but significantly slower and much more intellectually challenging!

The following day I woke to the ongoing noise of continually barking dogs. The roosters were also doing their thing and when the traffic kicked off and was joined by the dawn chorus I realized there was no escape.

It was a real pleasure to meet Michael Breen who has served the poor of Africa for many years. Originally from the Republic of Ireland, he was joining us for a week or so in Chitokoloki. He specialises in obstetric fistula surgery and while he has spent many years in Zambia he has now been displaced and heads up a unit in Madagascar funded by Anne Gloag who with her brother founded the international Stagecoach empire. Amazingly, Michael knew a surgeon from South Africa who started his specialist training with me in Glasgow in 1979.

We set off from Lusaka in the little Cessna and flew 3 hours to Sakeji, landed on the dirt strip there, deposited Andrew, took on some fuel and flew another hour and a half to Chitokoloki. It was great to connect with David McAdam and Joey Speichinger again. For the first time I met Alison Brundage and 13 week old Jack who had come to welcome his dad home. I was taken back to the nice house I had been given before and Lorraine McAdam had left some Arran Aromatics soap for me – a nice touch.

"One way to keep the population down"

I was well aware of the huge problem that surrounds the supply of blood for transfusion in Zambia. Some years before, international aid had helped to fund a new national transfusion service for Zambia. All donated blood in Zambia is tested for four transfusion transmissible infections namely HIV, Hepatitis B and C and syphilis. The World Health Organisation also recommends screening for the malaria parasite. Any unit of blood that tests positive for one of these infections is discarded. The remaining blood may be stored and made available to transfusion outlets many of which are in district hospitals. The WHO estimates that if 1% of the population of a country donate blood the country would be self-sufficient. However, in Zambia some 10% of blood donations are discarded because of one or other of the transfusion transmissible agents.[10] The result is that blood is in critically short supply. While the transfusion centres in Solwezi and Lusaka were set up to ensure protection for patients from transmissible viruses, the practice of using locally sourced blood, even in a life threatening emergency, is regarded as a punishable offence. Even in situations where urgent transfusion is considered essential to save life, it cannot be given – first because there is often no 'official' blood available and secondly because staff are threatened with dismissal if they stray from the nationally regulated policy and assist in the giving of un-cross-matched blood or even properly matched (but not virally screened), locally sourced blood. This policy is disastrous. Acute hospitals cannot function properly without blood. It would be hard to conceive a policy which would be more likely to lead to unnecessary deaths for the purpose of preventing conditions which now pose much less of a threat to life and health than they did a decade ago. Regulation trumps compassion and common sense. It caused me to think that while progress has been made in global surgery, a policy like this renders efficient and safe care impossible. We have a long way to go to counter this deranged situation. Pragmatism cannot be tolerated, it seems. The sooner those who protect this policy and threaten to criminalise health care workers who do everything in their power to avoid preventable deaths wake up to the reality, the better. It is clear that in a population threatened with chronic, anaemia producing, diseases like malaria and bilharzia, patients are prone to suffer a sudden and dramatic requirement for blood transfusion. The system is set up to fail as things stand and despite protestation and representation from individuals, hospitals and groups of hospitals it appears that the issue has reached an impasse. I wonder if it is time to make an international fuss and speak out in the medical press?

Pathology overload

Today was a day with a gynaecological flavour although virtually all the other medical and surgical disciplines surfaced at some point. There is no shortage of work!

Dr. Michael Breen, whilst originally from Dublin, has developed a unique and international expertise in the management of obstetric fistulas. He has even authored his own textbook, which he makes freely available. These fistulas which typically arise following a lengthy or complicated labour result in complete urinary incontinence. Many of the women are cast off by their husbands and consigned to a life of correctable misery. Like many parts of the world where obstetric care is inadequate there ends up being a reservoir of these VVF (vesico-vaginal fistula) patients in the community. The surgery to correct these is sometimes complex, difficult, and specialised but it can be highly effective. Michael is a master at treating these women and it was a pleasure to assist him for most of the day. Like most of his countrymen he is full of the Irish craic and not a few mnemonics, checklists and assorted quotations – "The better is the enemy of the good." We did a few fistulas as well as some other assorted uro-gynaecology procedures. A good learning experience for me! In between cases, I was invited to see some patients with the most advanced pathology imaginable. We have listed three total hysterectomies for endometrial or cervical cancer, one total cystectomy for bladder cancer, an enormous gastric ulcer, a left colon cancer, a host of hernias, sterilization procedures, stoma reversals, an amputation for diabetes and a large orbital tumour which will involve enucleation of the eye. Several patients were considered beyond repair – one with advanced cervical cancer, several with HIV including various complications and one awful case in a young woman with a huge complex and extensive dermoid tumour involving about 50% of her abdominal wall. It might be possible to remove the lesion although it would be a real challenge. We will likely need some plastic surgical input to swing the required tissue transfer flaps to cover the defect. We'll need some better imaging to attempt to plan the approach. More controlled violence will characterise tomorrow.

Raising the dead

The call went out – could we take a patient who had been attacked by a black mamba? Mambas are amongst the most deadly of the poisonous snakes. They are fast, aggressive, can raise themselves up and attack the upper body at speed. The poor patient in this incident was already dead but his family and friends knew that the hospital had an injection that could neutralise the effects of a snakebite and prove to be life saving. They took some persuading that there was little point in bringing a corpse to the hospital. Even the anti-venom, effective as it may be, is powerless to raise the dead. Too bad – it might have enhanced our reputation.

To be honest I feel a bit like needing raised myself. I normally have a robust constitution but felt nauseated and a bit faint in theatre this morning. I was in the midst of removing a horrible bulky eye and orbital tumour when a wave of nausea swept over me – I had to scrub out leaving David to get on with the case on his own while I went to lie down in the coffee room. I recognized the vaso-vagal signs, slow pulse, facial sweating and fortunately had the presence of mind to reach for a big enough receptacle to catch the contents of my stomach – it is amazing how the sense of feeling as though death might be a reasonable outcome can be completely transformed by a real good vomiting session.

Moses

Today was Michael Breen's last operating day so we did three cases together, a cystectomy for bladder cancer, a hysterectomy for a fibroid uterus and an ovarian cyst. He has been good fun – typical Irish chat and good sense of humour. He shared my house here and I will miss the fact that he set the breakfast table every morning and made the tea and toast. Very civilised.

When I got going today, I still felt the remains of the illness which floored me yesterday. Risked a single slice of toast for breakfast and felt progressively better as the day went on.

We spent the rest of the day sorting out a list of surgical cases for the next few weeks. The most poignant moment came at the very tail end of the day. I was introduced to Moses – aged 5. He had the most awful facial tumour imaginable. It is hard to conceive that anything could be done to deal with this. He came marching up to me – full of energy and shook my hand like an old friend. His eye is long gone and one glance at the image of his face will tell more than I could ever describe.

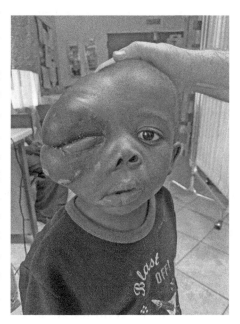

A sad reminder

So many patients have problems for which there is just no good solution – at least not in rural Zambia. Terrible corneal injuries, dreadful burns, advanced tumours, inoperable jaundice, infertility from pelvic inflammatory disease, HIV, cirrhosis, profound stroke and today, two patients with quadriplegia – one of whom, a young woman sustained an unstable fracture of her neck following a fall from an ox cart and is now on skull traction with metal tongs like a pair of pincers set into her skull. This looks very strange but is wonderfully effective – she even appears to have regained a measure of limited movement despite her spinal cord trauma.

Once again the most poignant moment came towards the end of the day. A young woman arrived by ambulance; twelve weeks pregnant but bleeding and thought to be miscarrying. She was brought into theatre where she delivered her dead foetus – it was about 6 inches long lying still on the operating table, complete with placenta. The baby was fully formed, all fingers and toes tiny but developed, as was its miniature face and features. I wonder how the pro-choice advocates would react to seeing the likes of this and facing the reality that while aborting a baby at that stage may be characterised in some kind of positive light as 'pro-choice,' it is nevertheless undeniably the deliberate taking of a baby's life. We can throw around the arguments in political debate until we are blue in the face but how can baby killing such as is considered legal across the Western world ever be considered moral or acceptable? It beggars belief.

Weird and Wonderful

The hospital here is like a strange museum of the most weird and obscure diagnoses one could imagine. I made a tour of all the patients in both the acute hospital and the Old Hospital today. Much of the diagnostic detail continues to be educated guesswork but at least it provides a strategy for onward decision making. Once again every discipline was represented. From the insane psychotics to serious trauma, from nephrotic syndrome to noma – a kind of oro-facial gangrene, from chronic joint swelling and dermatitis herpetiformis, to contractures and from jaundice due to cholangiocarcinoma to congenital anomalies, not to mention the patients who are recovering from surgery and those with malaria, bilharzia, hydrocephalus, goitre, parotid tumours, broken limbs, fungal infections, cerebral palsy and even a young woman who tried (almost successfully) to hang herself; she was cut down and resuscitated just before she was strangled. To top it all – a variation on the west of Scotland theme of sharp abdominal trauma – a guy was shipped in by ambulance from

Lukulu having been attacked by a spear. A doctor in the local hospital operated on him, removed the spear, repaired a perforated small bowel and sent him to Chit for further management. Now normally an operation for a penetrating abdominal injury would involve a large abdominal incision and a full exploration of the abdomen. This chap came with a mini incision in the mid abdomen through which only a very limited assessment would have been possible. There were no notes! We had no idea how much he bled or what the detailed injuries were. The only technical detail with respect to the intestinal injury was that it was "done." I assume that they made an attempt to repair some damage. Amazingly, he had a reasonable blood pressure, slight fever, a rapid pulse rate and he seemed warm and well perfused. I decided to watch him overnight but would not have been at all surprised if we ended up taking him to theatre to have a man-sized incision and a proper look. In Glasgow, I have encountered abdominal wounds from guns, machetes, axes, swords and knives – never a spear. I hope the idea does not catch on.

Last night, I had time for a wander down to the River Zambezi before dark. This is the dry season so the flood plains are accessible. I rapidly acquired a following of small children who were inclined to exhaust their entire English vocabulary by continually enquiring: "How are yooo?" I walked past some bathing areas, avoiding the cattle and pigs that were roaming around and made for the rapids where the river bed drops its level by only a couple of feet. This seems to be a relatively safe and shallow area so at least one would expect to see any approaching predators. There were plenty of dug out canoes and it soon became clear that there was a major local sporting contest in process nearby. The Chitokoloki Celtics were playing a friendly match against a team from "across" – the term they use to refer to any community on the other side of the river. So the team from Chihungu, decked out in sky blue, was taking on the local soccer heroes. A large crowd had gathered having walked for about half an hour from the village to give support. Not only was there a referee, there were two linesmen who demonstrated consistently poor judgment and enthusiastically waved their makeshift flags. There was even a commentator. There was no amplification of course, just this slightly odd chap with an apparent degree of cognitive impairment, wandering up and down the line providing a running commentary at the top of his voice on what he thought was happening on the pitch.

A slow day

I spent part of Saturday preparing to make a contribution at the church. Beyond that there was a Caesarian section and not much else. It was a good day to enjoy the sun and catch up on some reading.

On Sunday I made a trip with David to Zambezi to visit a local church there. We received a lovely welcome and there were around 50 in attendance. It was a good chance to share and they were very keen to send their greetings to their fellow Christians in Scotland. After the service they insisted on serving us lunch. We washed our hands with water from a bucket, which a nice man poured over our hands as we washed with soap. The menu comprised chicken, rice, nshima, liver, some greens and bottles of full fat Coke! A lump of nshima can hold an average person down in the seat for about three hours before the feeling of abdominal fullness begins to abate. It is not very high in calories and certainly not rich in nutritional value. It is difficult to convey what it is really like but it is not dissimilar to a big lump of dense solid porridgy stodge. Not for those with a sensitive or refined palate!

Ingenuity and bravery required

Some days progress without any discernible structure. Today we dealt with a young chap who sustained a nasty mid shaft fracture of right tibia and fibula whilst playing football. The injury was compound in that the bone had protruded through the skin. They had made an attempt at putting a splint on but might as well have used a hankie for all the good it did. Now he is in a hefty long leg plaster so hopefully that will sort him out. My friend Chambula – the Manchester United supporting teacher and relatively recently recognized village headman - came off his motorbike about 6 weeks ago breaking his forearm and mincing his face so required lots of suturing. He was hoping for release from his cast but unfortunately there is little sign of new bone formation so he is sentenced to immobility for a bit longer. Because his arm is in plaster he is not allowed to fulfil his role as a teacher. It is not clear to me why that should be the case. However, I suspect he is rather enjoying his time off. The rest of the day was filled with clinic patients of all shapes and sizes.

We also had a more careful look at wee Moses – the boy with the big facial tumour. He presented a real dilemma. Without surgery it is inevitable that this lesion will take his life as it gradually grows. We have resolved to have a go at removing it, despite the risks.

Two more visitors arrived today – Johnny Dalton, a newly qualified doctor from Cardiff University. He has been working in Belfast for the past year and he arrived with his medical student wife, Hannah. She will be here for 4 weeks – Johnny for only a fortnight. It is interesting to see the reaction of new people to the avalanche of pathology and organised chaos that is Chitokoloki. No wonder people feel like they are kind of caught in the headlights until coping mechanisms kick in.

At the end of the day, I had a wander along the track that leads out of the village towards Zambezi. It is just a dirt road, no tarmac in sight. Vehicles of any kind are rare. I think one car passed me in about half an hour and clouds of dust followed it, of course. There were plenty of people wandering around. All of them are really very friendly. The little children kind of gape at the strange white man and sometimes look a bit horrified and scared. Some were ready to come for a chat or walk along to keep pace with me for some of the way. Almost all of them were dressed in rags – many of them utterly filthy and worn. Few have proper shoes – most have plastic flip flops and the houses scattered along the track are simple huts – some made from grass and thatch and others from mud brick. In downtown Chitokoloki there are a few scattered and rather pathetic shops and the occasional flimsy house. Sometimes a closer inspection reveals something quite incongruous. Much of the scene would be as it was a century ago with the exception of the small photovoltaic solar panel mounted on a thatched roof. Every self respecting African millennial needs some method of charging his cell phone! Despite the utter poverty mobile phones have become a common accessory.

Partial lunar eclipse

So today was a day for some old fashioned cancer surgery. Dorcas is a lady in her fifties who came with severe anaemia – a haemoglobin level running at less than half the value it should be.

She has a large palpable mass in her abdomen and I was able to colonoscope her last week to confirm the diagnosis of a big bulky left colon cancer. We were in her room discussing how much blood to try to give her prior to surgery. I was telling one of the students about the possible nightmare scenario which sometimes arises in the UK if a patient will not accept blood or blood products because they follow the teaching of the Jehovah's Witnesses and that rather ties the clinicians hands, not to mention putting the patient at significantly increased risk. Well, I could hardly believe it – having had that discussion on the "what if" scenario – the bold Dorcas announced that she was indeed a Jehovah's Witness and would not accept blood. Happily David was able to talk sense to her and strangely enough she agreed to accept only packed red cells. This was a good result because what she needed was packed red cells. Normally blood is presented as whole blood in Zambia not as packed cells so we had to encourage the lab to present her blood in a form as close to packed cells as possible to make it acceptable. She had her surgery with minimal blood loss and we gave her two units of blood to aid her recovery – the blood was due to expire the same day so at least we got some use out of it.

We had a few minor cases that I did with Johnny who is likely to pursue a surgical career so enjoyed getting a piece of the action. We then tackled a large sarcoma on an upper arm – a solid tumour about the size of a small rugby ball arising from deep in the bulk of the biceps muscle. This was quite a challenge – ending up right down on the periosteum of the mid shaft of the humerus. However, it was carved out leaving no tumour behind although I was nervous that some of the nerves running close to the lesion may well have compromised his wrist and hand function. As his ketamine wore off the patient was up for a fight so I was delighted to see his elbow, wrist and finger flexors all working with no problem.

I was about to turn in for the night when I was called to go back to the hospital – Dr Ros was presiding over chaos! Two new emergency patients, both young men, had arrived. One had HIV and bad pneumonia – a real candidate for one of the very threatening but weird infections that AIDS patients can get and these can be difficult to treat. The other chap looked like he had peritonitis and would likely need to go to theatre. However, at that point, pain killers, antibiotics and support was the best policy and he would be reviewed later. No wonder Jenni once described this place as 'mental'; it lived up to that description today.

Wandering back from the hospital there was an obvious partial lunar eclipse. Opportunities to pick out structures in the night sky are unparalleled and this was impressive and easy to see.

Double crossed

The following day the chap admitted with acute abdominal pain was no better. It was a typical acute abdomen with a very atypical explanation. Not only did he turn out to have a sigmoid volvulus with about 2 feet of gangrenous large bowel, he also had the very curious arrangement involving the small intestine as well. This was not a straightforward twisted segment of gut (a volvulus) - this was a rare double volvulus. So in addition to a length of dead large bowel there was a 5-foot segment of discontinuous small bowel that was also necrotic. It proved impossible to disentangle this without dividing the bowel whilst all the time attempting to prevent the possibility of any blood draining out of the dead segment of gut and potentially back into the circulation. I was later to learn that this condition is well described in tropical surgery but I have never come across anything quite like it. It was as if the mesentery of the small bowel and the sigmoid were knotted together. It was quite impossible to disentangle this without literally cutting through the intestine close to the apex of the 'knot.' It was then possible to free the twists and knots and we were left with 2 loops of bowel to reconstruct. The lower-most section was divided and dropped back into the pelvis. The other end was brought out as a stoma and the small bowel was joined back together again.

The surgical action concluded with a large dental abscess that also needed surgery and so an old fashioned incision and drainage was performed resulting in much laudable pus!

We closed out the day with some amateur astronomy. Light pollution is not a problem here. There are no lights worth speaking about after the sun goes down at about 6:30pm. This evening we took the opportunity of lining up David's telescope on Jupiter to try and see all four moons. This was an amazing new experience for me. Saturn, complete with its ring, was also clearly visible. David was able to regale a few of us with a fair volume of astronomical trivia. So we are now all armed with the details of the orbital speed of the Earth, the moon, Venus and Mercury. Note to self - there is much of interest to see in the clear night sky. As one who has had no more than an ability to identify the likes of the Great Bear and Sagittarius, seeing the moons of Jupiter was a revelation.

'Chachiwahi'

A good day but powerless surgery! The hospital electricity supply is normally very secure. However, since the source is solar energy it has to be rendered usable by means of an inverter. The system appeared to be overheating perhaps because of a malfunctioning fan. For most of the day we had either no power or very limited power. That meant no ventilator, no suction, no light and limited oxygen.

Surgeons are forever complaining about the position of the operating light. Light, it turns out, is an over-rated luxury in the bush. We completed the first cases today without light or power. Mercifully all went well. Bilateral hernias and a bilateral tubal ligation followed by some agricultural urology to find a route into the bladder of a nice old boy with a tight narrowed segment in his prostatic urethra. After the power came back on we managed to remove a big thyroid lesion. I was reminded just how vascular the neck can be. It more than explains how people can bleed out from a neck wound.

We then managed some endoscopies and oesophageal dilatations before finishing the surgical hostilities with another gynaecological case – there seems to be a never ending supply of gynaecological problems! This woman had a big semi-cystic swelling close to her right ovary. I did a laparotomy and took it out – it was a classic dermoid; a big 10x12x8cm partly cystic lump which when opened contained a big chunk of hair, some other skin remnants and a tooth. Very strange, but very benign, so she should do well. The rest of the day has been distorted because of the acute lack of blood. Essentially we were unable to safely complete any more major abdominal surgery until the situation is rectified. The mission plane is off to Lusaka today so hopefully will return with some blood supplies.

Poverty and misery

I am constantly surprised by the way people seem to accept their fate here. We have quite a few people who are receiving palliative care in the form of minimal symptomatic support. Those with liver failure from advanced primary liver cancer or bilharzia appear not to have unrealistic expectations. This is just as well because there is precious little that can be done for them. On a positive note – the major cases I operated on earlier in the week are all doing well – even the young chap with the double volvulus seemed better today. Today I saw a woman with severe liver disease. One of the features is the accumulation of fluid in the abdominal cavity. In her case she appeared to be very heavily pregnant but the swelling was all fluid. So much fluid, in fact, that she was much, much bigger than one would ever expect even at full term pregnancy. She was so disabled and distressed by this that we have resolved to get hold of some shunts; some of these very severe cases can be dramatically improved by an operation to create a kind of shunt to allow this overproduction of fluid in the abdomen to be diverted away into the circulation where the kidneys can process it and relieve the pressure. I remember doing one of these procedures here on a previous visit and the result was apparently very good. I hoped we would be able to really help this poor, pathetic soul as well.

I went for a walk today leaving Chitokoloki on the only navigable road and headed north. There is simply bush all around. Every 300-400 yards there would be a clutch of simple, desperately poor, African mud brick or straw houses. The people are always ready to recognize the strange white man with a ready smile, a wave or a: "Hallo, how are you? I am fine. How are you?" That is about as far as their English will go but then my command of Lunda or Luvale is not even that good. I can say the words for 'pain', 'good' and 'tomorrow' and that is about it! Several of my new acquaintances were up for a chat. One wanted advice about the fact that his recently broken leg was still sore and he hobbled along beside me for a few hundred yards until I had served his purposes. Another introduced himself as "Miracle" (his last name was long and unpronounceable) and told me that he was really cool! He certainly had the chat, the swagger and the attitude and wanted to know all sorts of information about Scotland and, amongst other things, what I was doing in Africa. I ended up walking for about two hours in total considering how nice it would be to know what they really think of the foreigners who come to this remote part of the world.

The highlight of the evening was finally being able to connect with Jenni in Glenshee, and Christine with Lynda in Birmingham by video call. It was the first time to make a decent family connection in two weeks!

Peace and quiet

The weekend was peppered by a few hospital visits but nothing desperate so no significant medical action. It was good to welcome James Elliot who arrived to join the maintenance team for 3 weeks. He is 18 and lives in Holland and expected to be erecting fences and doing other heavy duty work while he is here. He had just completed a gap year and had acquired useful joinery and building skills by working with a construction company in Holland. Sunday comprised of more church meetings than I think I have ever attended in one day. There were two services in Chit this morning followed by a village service in Chambula Village nearby, followed by an English service back in Chit. Then this evening we met in Dr Ros' house for another session so all in all it has hardly been a day of rest. Interspersed with all of this was a very nice roast beef lunch and a couple of hospital visits to assess patients who were newly admitted and causing concern. At least by then we had some blood supplies although power was still a bit of an issue. I was left hoping that it could be fixed soon.

Indescribable tragedy

About a month's worth of pathology reports arrived by email and amidst a typical clinic notably free from malingerers we spent some time marrying results with case records and deciding which patients needed to be called back to discuss further treatment. Getting histo-pathological analysis of biopsy material or surgical specimens is a major problem. A very kind Christian pathologist called Ian Gibson processes these samples. He is based in Winnipeg so by the time someone leaving Chit is able to arrange to send the tissue samples to Western Canada and Ian has a chance to process them and then study the microscope slides and prepare a report, it is not unusual for two or three months to have passed between taking a sample and receiving the opinion. When I was training in surgical oncology I spent some time in one of the world's foremost cancer hospitals, the Memorial Sloan Kettering Cancer Center in New York City. It is a hospital for cancer and allied diseases. Every now and again there would be a biopsy result on a suspected malignancy which proved to be negative – a reason to celebrate one of the allied diseases! There are precious few examples of allied diseases here. This is a hotbed of cancer diagnoses. Only one of our reports was a surprising example of a suspected malignancy that turned out to be a false alarm. Of the remainder – some had already been adequately treated, some needed more work and quite a few were beyond hope. Even the second and third line treatment options available in the West are not accessible to patients here. Sometimes even the prospect of a long overland journey to Lusaka is no guarantee of appropriate care.

It has almost been a pattern that the last clinic patient of the day presents a particularly unforgettable story. A middle aged woman was gently led in by her husband. It was quickly apparent that she had real difficulty in seeing – in fact she had lost all light perception in both eyes over a very short period of time. There are not many conditions that will produce this effect. Often you can identify the cause of loss of vision on careful clinical examination together with ophthalmoscopy (that's the use of the curious instrument the optician uses to get uncomfortably close and peer into the back of your eye) or even the use of a slit lamp. This lady's eyes appeared normal. No cataract, no retinal detachment or retinal artery occlusion. She actually had perfectly normal looking eyes but without a vestige of vision. This was a classic case where the doctor sees nothing and the patient sees nothing and the diagnosis was retrobulbar neuritis. The cause was unknown in this case but, sadly, there was nothing that could be done. It was little wonder that she shed silent tears as this tragic news unfolded. The couple left the clinic devoid of any support. No agencies, Royal Societies or National Institutes, no specialist nurses – no meaningful help of any kind. They come from many kilometres away so, without hope of improvement, they headed off into the fading light of evening, a protective husband carefully guiding his permanently non-seeing wife. This was undoubtedly one of the saddest moments of my time here.

The only other similar example I heard about here concerned a woman who had a relatively mild eye complaint and consulted the local witch doctor. The people seem scared of these characters (and with good reason). The influence of spells and witchcraft forms part of a blame network here about which the only good thing from our point of view is that it is racist and seems not to apply to the white people. This woman was treated by an unbelievable technique. The witch doctor poured battery acid into both of her eyes permanently damaging the cornea and blinding her for life. When she heard the outlook she was beside herself in anger and distress. Would they ever report or complain about the witch doctor? Not a chance! The culture is based on fear and these dangerous charlatans continue to peddle their evil influence across the community. Infuriating!

Moon talk

Gordon asked a question of the staff at their meeting this morning (23rd July). He wondered if anyone knew which event had taken place fifty years ago this week and was being celebrated in the world's press and media. No one knew. None of the local folks from Chitokoloki had any notion about the lunar landings on July 24th 1969. Admittedly many of them would not even have been born. Nevertheless, they do seem to know about other personalities who seem rather inconsequential in the grand scheme of things. Even when the explanation and the story of Neil Armstrong and Buzz Aldrin was told, most of them seemed totally non-plussed. Maybe it's my age but I remember thinking that it was one of the most significant events in human history and I even remember when the Apollo 8 astronauts (Anders, Lovell and Borman) read from Genesis 1 as they orbited the moon on Christmas Eve 1968. It just emphasised to me how the entire focus here goes little further than the confines of this community. Many of the folks who live here will never even go to other Zambian centres such as Lusaka, Livingstone or the copper belt. The vast majority would never ever have the wherewithal to travel anywhere, not that they are any less content as a result.

Our operating schedule today was again interrupted by power problems. We did, however, manage to reverse a stoma by means of a laparotomy on a nineteen year old lad who was convinced it would never happen. We also removed a thyroid lobe as well as fixing two baby hernias and performing some urological hocus pocus by widening tubes that have become narrowed for various reasons.

The two local men, Kayumbo and Jack, who are essential to the functioning of the operating theatre; finding stuff, cleaning, sterilising and packing instruments and gowns, are such pleasant fellows. Nothing is too much trouble "Doc!" When they are nowhere to be seen I just have to call "Kayumbo!" or "Jack!" and they materialise ready to find, fetch or help in whatever way they can. They inhabit a kind of utility space where there are layers of chaotic shelves with tubes, catheters, instruments, laundry, boxes of supplies and all manner of things. It has kind of become known as Jack's box and so the cry goes up; "Is Jack in his box?" He usually is and is ready to come and do whatever is necessary, take photos, translate into the local vernacular, obtain consent, locate a particular instrument or patient or case record or anaesthetic agent. They are even ready to scrub and assist at surgery. They are multi-talented and indispensable. It is a real wonder to see these guys in action. So what qualifications do they have? In this context it is not even a meaningful question!

Tomorrow, I plan to tackle a shunt procedure in the most swollen and fluid filled abdomen I have ever encountered in my entire career. Talk about dodgy – this is a bit dodgy. One can only hope that it works out well.

Get it in the jugular

The power issues have been bypassed now and await a definitive solution. A special component is on its way from Dublin to get the power inverter working normally again. The family of a young missionary couple is coming out from Belfast via Dublin over the next few days and they will be bringing the necessary equipment. It is just as well that Chit has a good number of diverse visitors.

As for the patient with the swollen abdomen, I have rarely seen such a thin patient – just a rickle of bones. She is 58 and at surgery we drew off a total of 15 litres of fluid and inserted a special tube to shunt the remaining fluid together with that which will inevitably continue to accumulate over the next few days, into the circulation via the internal jugular vein. It is quite an elegant procedure, exploiting a good idea and while in principle the plumbing is quite straightforward it is impressive for observers and carries a little risk in exposing the lower end of the jugular vein at the root of the neck. With such a thin patient it was a lesson in text-book anatomy with a view of the cervical fascia, the phrenic nerve and the carotid artery as well as the vein itself. Everything went smoothly. The surprise came at the end of the procedure. The swelling had gone. The shunt was nicely positioned. However, the patient's abdominal wall was so pathetically thin that one could see the loops of bowel within the abdomen through the skinny muscle coat and to top it off her spleen which was not detectable before now sits up like an internal rugby ball sticking up into the left upper quadrant. She is in for a shock! At least she will be pleased that she has lost close to 16kg (approximately 2 and a half stones) and will be able to move around and breathe much more comfortably. Occasionally, surgeons can take the credit for making a dramatic difference. Let's hope it is durable.

Goran the Serb

Goran Jovic is something of a surgical celebrity in Africa. Everyone seems to know him. He is linked with colleagues in most of the African countries. He claims to be the best plastic surgeon in Zambia. In reality, he is the only plastic surgeon in Zambia, so his claim is understandable. He also has friends in the former Yugoslavia, the UK, including Glasgow where he is a Fellow of the Royal College of Physicians and Surgeons, and he is also known in Boston and elsewhere in the USA. Based at the University Teaching Hospital (UTH) in Lusaka, he is quick to point out that while Chitokoloki can be characterised by organised chaos, UTH can genuinely boast the disorganised variety.

Goran arrived in Africa when the war in Yugoslavia broke out and he has made his career in Lusaka but also helps to provide a service in lots of peripheral hospitals on an entirely charitable basis under the auspices of Flyspec. He has a pilot's licence and frequently flies himself in to a mission station, runs a clinic and an operating list and then flies on.

An entire team arrived with Goran today and consisted of two newly retired consultants from the West of Scotland together with Colin West, an orthopaedic surgeon from Lusaka. They set about seeing a large number of patients who had come from far and wide and by 9:30pm when they retreated for something to eat the consultation headcount came to 85 patients. While that clinic was progressing I assisted Goran with an attempt to reconstruct the face of a child where much of the central section had been destroyed by noma. We also carried out some skin grafting for Monica, a lovely young girl of 7 years of age who survived extensive burns. Her clothes caught fire as she was walking past some burning vegetation. The only area spared has been her head and neck. Her back had healed well but her thighs, abdomen, arms and flanks were still raw and she has now donated most of the skin of her legs as skin grafts to cover these areas.

Some twenty orthopaedic cases were prepared for surgery the following day and even with two theatres running and two surgeons operating they kept going from 7am until late into the evening. While the orthopaedic team were fully occupied in theatre, it allowed the rest of us to make a more leisurely visit to the remaining patients. Monica was 'a bit fine' that morning which was pleasing. Actually, it is almost miraculous that she survived at all. Had she been treated in Lusaka, Goran reckoned her chance of survival would be negligible. The afternoon was a chance to relax so I went walkabout with my camera and spent the evening preparing for some talks I need to give on Sunday as well as enjoying the hospitality of some of the permanent mission team members here. We have been very well fed and entertained. Meanwhile, having been boasting of his prowess as an angler, Goran went fishing on the river and caught - nothing! Serves him right!

Question of the day!

We had planned an ambitious programme for the following day. First, was to operate on a huge desmoid tumour, then the

5-year-old Moses with his large mesenchymal facial cancer and finally a patient with a longstanding burn contracture. This plan was not really practical and would again have involved two teams of surgeons, a luxury that did not exist. The major worry was that as we had little or no blood, the risk of an operative death was real for both of the tumour patients. Without surgery, the prospect will mean certain death for both so an operation, however risky, is their only chance of survival. This is a difficult dilemma for any family to have to face.

As for the question of the day? David was keen to ask a real tester. Quite often his questions concern some diagnostic dilemma but it is equally likely that the topic could be astronomical trivia or would give him the chance to pass on a nugget of astonishing insight. Today the category was close to the latter variety. He posed his question: 'What is the most useful gift you can give to a leper in Africa?' Bear in mind that leprosy is a terribly disabling condition and sufferers risk losing fingers, toes and more as the disease progresses. While the condition is now becoming less and less common, we did see a leprosy patient today, which was the context for the question. I sensed from the mischievous glint in his eye as he kept the assembled company waiting, that the answer would contain an element of surprise. It did. The answer was – a cat! Why? Simply because, if they own a cat, it can keep the rats at bay. One of the reasons these patients lose tissue is because their homes are rat infested and because of peripheral nerve damage a leper will often have no sensation in their digits. Rats, therefore, can come and nibble or gnaw at their extremities hence the tissue damage. A cat will keep the rats away and preserve tissue. Logical!

A fateful decision

One of the lovely unwritten traditions at Chitokoloki is that when visitors arrive or leave from the airstrip as many personnel as are free make their way to the hangar to bid them welcome or farewell as appropriate. I set off for the airstrip first thing this morning to bid farewell to a couple of visitors who were heading for Livingstone and Lusaka for their flights back to Europe.

Since Goran the Plastic Surgeon was still here, we decided to do a combined procedure and remove the facial / orbital tumour from the diminutive Moses. We all had our misgivings because this was clearly going to be a major undertaking and fraught with danger. Moses was the youngest of seven siblings and he had come all the way from Angola. He had been in Chitokoloki being assessed and prepared for potential surgery for the last three months. His father, who has left most of his other children in Angola, accompanied him. Moses' future was desperate. Without surgery he faced a certain and awful death as the tumour advanced and so our judgment was that a chance of surgical resection might help prolong his life and at least could give him reasonable palliation. There was always the risk of a death on the operating table as a result of blood loss and when you only weight 20kg – it doesn't take an enormous loss of blood to produce a significant threat. The operation went well and the tumour was removed. Unfortunately it proved impossible to get rid of some microscopic disease, which had invaded the outer table of his skull, and so even his major surgery (a maxillectomy and radical excision of the orbit) would not have cured the problem. Without sophisticated scans the only way we could make that determination was at a stage of the operation well beyond the surgical point of no return. As we were preparing to raise a scalp flap to cover the large defect in his face he rapidly deteriorated and suffered a cardiac arrest on the table. With CPR, atropine, adrenaline and blood we were able to restore a good heart rhythm after about 8 minutes. His oxygen levels remained satisfactory throughout but this insult contributed to a further deterioration and he became acidotic and cooled down – a fateful combination. Again he required CPR and again became stable following resuscitation. The final insult was a failure of his blood clotting. In the face of haemorrhage followed by the transfusion of three units of stored blood together with intravenous fluids; the stage is set for the production of a coagulopathy. This occurs because the supply of clotting proteins becomes exhausted and the only ways to correct the problem are either to give clotting factors, fresh frozen plasma or freshly donated whole blood. Despite giving him fresh O negative blood (donated as an emergency by one of the missionaries) he sustained a further arrest and we struggled to maintain a cardiac output until finally his system succumbed and poor Moses passed away. To deal with a death on the operating table is never easy and it seemed especially difficult when it looked as though the worst of the procedure was past. Once again it emphasised how the lack of adequate laboratory support and the lack of blood products can be such an enormous problem. Everyone left theatre after more than 12 hours, feeling dejected at the sad outcome. The decision we made was risky and fateful and the question remains as to whether it was right. There is a fine line between life and death and in this case the thing that took me by surprise was how his circulation, which had been stable in the face of a serious challenge, quickly collapsed. That his heart was strong was the reason he rallied and seemed to make a recovery. However, the surgical trauma complicated by massive bleeding proved too much. A sad day.

Bush burial

I stopped off briefly in the hospital to see a new admission with puerperal fever. This is a condition, previously called childbed fever, which Semmelweis the famous Hungarian obstetrician dealt with in Vienna in the 1840s and largely eradicated it by means of a policy of careful hand hygiene. It has virtually gone from the scene in the UK. However, it still kills young women following childbirth in Africa and the girl we saw and scanned with a portable ultrasound machine was as septic as could be, to the point that her life was genuinely in danger. She had delivered at home in her village and we checked that she had no sign of a retained placenta and then filled her up with antibiotics. We also had a look at a young distressed agitated boy who was almost certainly in the early stages of liver failure. The most likely cause was hepatitis but we had no way of easily proving that. He received the best supportive care we could give and all we could do was hope that he might begin to show some signs of recovery.

I was glad to have made video contact with home today. It was really great to see everyone, especially, of course, my dear wife! I was particularly encouraged and thankful to see my grandchildren, Jaz (7), Isla (5) and Anya (2) – each a picture of health, especially in the wake of the events of yesterday when we lost wee Moses, aged only 5, on the operating table.

After attending and contributing to the church service this morning with the help of Mr Mukwasio who translated my talk into Lunda, we enjoyed lunch provided by Dr Ros Jefferson. Ros, as well as being a high-energy paediatrician, is a superb cook and a wonderful hostess. Once again today she was able to demonstrate her culinary skills. Immediately after lunch we headed for the mortuary to support those who gathered to be with Moses' family. We followed the funeral procession across the airstrip to see his simple coffin buried during a short graveside service. The funeral was conducted by Jack, our theatre assistant. He gave a message emphasising the importance of having the real hope that only the Christian message can bring in the face of death. He spoke well, with compassion and concern for Moses' father who was distraught. I hope it provided some comfort for him and for Moses' older brother who was able to attend.

After that – I walked for miles listening to some podcasts and before dark watched the local 'Young Stars' give the 'Chitokoloki Celtic' a sound 10-0 beating on the football pitch. A round of golf would be just the thing. However, there is no chance. The nearest course is 569 km and an eight and a half hour drive away. I hope I can remember how to swing a club when I get back.

Filling the gap

As I sent tales of life in Chit back to the UK, the feedback was sometimes quite surprising. It is odd how extraordinary circumstances and events seen to become less and less remarkable. People who hear or read the tales from a Western perspective not only have little concept about the reality of life in rural Africa, they are often bemused by the nature of the activity with all its frenzied and dramatic variety. Today seemed like any other operating day. In reality it was absolutely nothing like any other Western operating day! There was the usual large queue of patients waiting at the door – all hoping that their turn would materialise. Having been added to the list, they show up day after day, hoping that we can get them treated. However, there was still no blood for transfusion so given the risk in taking on major procedures in patients, some of whom have a blood count in their boots, these were evidently going to have to wait rather longer than they would like.

There are several distinctives that exist in sharp contrast to any other hospital in which I have worked. The entire ethos in Chitokoloki is based around medical missionary work – a desire to communicate the Christian message of the importance of faith in Christ and a demonstration of Christian concern by the provision of free medical care (as well as the opportunity to serve the community in multiple other ways). The full time missionaries are driven by the desire to demonstrate God's love for people by investing their time, effort, resources and energy. I am completely supportive of these objectives and I am full of admiration for the way in which they have sacrificed the opportunity to have a lucrative and comfortable career in the West to serve the poor of Africa. I already described the practice of praying with a patient as they are being prepared for operation. This appears to be completely natural for the Zambian patients, no awkward or embarrassed reaction, just a real appreciation of the care being shown to them and an eagerness to invoke God's help in the most threatening of circumstances. In Western culture it is always interesting to note how the hard nosed atheism and bravado that so often characterises life in general tends to dissolve away in the face of a threatening illness. It should be no surprise that people will seek the help of a power greater than themselves when life goes out of control and they stare mortality in the face. In Chitokoloki, day after day you find the reality of genuine Christian love in practical action. It is well worth supporting.

Fright of my life!

Mercifully, there hasn't been much night work for me on this visit. Because we start at 7:30am each day at the hospital I find myself crawling off to bed about 9:30pm. So when the phone rang at 1am it was a rude awakening indeed. A patient in labour had failed to progress in the second stage. The baby's head remained high and showed no signs of shifting. A Caesarian section was the obvious answer. We did a quick scan to identify the position of the placenta and had the baby out and yelling in under 10 minutes. That was all well and good. I have never found it easy to get back to sleep after a night peppered by some surgical action but on this occasion the operation had been so stress free that, as I wandered the 400 yards back home in the pitch dark, I was confident that sleep would not be far away. How wrong that proved to be! I got to within about 100 yards of my house and I got the fright of my life. Some animal ran at me from behind at full speed. Suddenly I heard it racing up behind me. I spun around wearing a headlight and the beast veered away. There was no barking but I could see its eyes shining green as it reflected my light and watched me from about 30 feet away. I reckoned it was probably a dog but it was impossible to see in the pitch darkness. My heart was suddenly racing. It is well known that there are rabid dogs around here so despite my trust in the NHS rabies vaccine I definitely did not relish the idea of getting on the wrong side of some aggressive beast. By the time I reached my door my heart rate was still clattering along at over 100 beats per minute. Sleep came - but not promptly.

Inexplicable stupidity

The community here tend to take recourse to local healers and local 'village' medicine rather than coming to the hospital for treatment. They use some kind of potent concoction of herbs to induce labour and it certainly seems to accelerate the process dramatically and in a totally uncontrolled way. To treat troublesome wounds, they will often 'consult' the local witch doctor - even patients who ought to know better will do this under duress from the family. The end result is often a load of chatta marks or superficial skin scars made by old razor blades and the problem is often compounded because they will then rub all sorts of non sterile material into the wounds. The 'medicaments' might include soot or ash, manure, soil, acid - little wonder that the outcome is sometimes dreadful. Gas gangrene or horrendous sepsis can be significant risks. It is sometimes the case that the only outcome might be amputation, blindness or even death. These witch doctors should be locked up but they are rarely caught or punished. There is a culture of genuine fear that going against the local healer will result in a bewitching and no one wants a spell cast upon them. All of this is doubly frustrating for the medical mission because not only is there physical help here but spiritual help is also freely available. Even professing African Christians find themselves caught up in this battle.

Likely lads

I was walking in downtown Chitokoloki today and as is routinely true just about everyone you meet says: "Hello" or: "How are you?" The technique I have developed is to simply greet someone coming the other way with a wave or by attempting to use the gentle handclapping Zambian greeting rather than trying to get into a conversation. A different policy threatens to end up in a potentially endless series of "How are you?" conversations, as follows.

'Stranger: "Hello, how are you?"

Me: "Fine, how are you?"

Stranger: "I am fine and how are you?"

Me: "I am fine" – note the attempt to conclude the exchange; but to no avail.

Stranger: "I am fine too, and how are you?" There is no escape!

As I explored the area, I met all sorts of folk who wanted to chat. One chap called James wants nothing other than for me to give him my tee-shirt. I don't mind leaving some clothes here but I was not about to whip off my shirt and make the donation right there and then! I also met Jack, the theatre orderly who does a sterling job in the hospital. He was cycling along the main road, which is just a sandy dirt track, on a very shiny new bike. He was insistent that I tried it out so that caused a bit of a stir. Even having returned the bike I had rapidly acquired a following of about dozen scrawny bedraggled looking kids who tracked me the rest of the way as I headed for the river. It was there that I came across two likely lads both in their late teens. Both had ridiculous hairstyles but I suppose no more ridiculous that we see in Scotland these days. One, Innocent by name (but I doubt, by nature) had a kind of home-made coloured stripe running obliquely from the front to the back of his head. He was keen to swap his big blingy watch for the nice gold watch my wife had given me for a significant birthday. I politely declined this

generous offer. The other, Dennis, was just as bright, friendly and talkative as his friend and he too had a very curious spiky hair style, not unlike the kind of look that some Premiership footballers display. I asked them if they liked football. They were very excited to tell me that they both played for the Chitokoloki Celtics and that they were playing this Saturday. They suggested that I come to watch and be ready to play if they needed me. I was flattered but will manage to resist the temptation of getting too involved. They also wanted me to give them sports socks and if possible a ball. I planned to go to the match – it promised to be entertaining for sure especially if past experience is anything to go by.

The baby killers are active

Zambia has quite strict laws about abortion. There is a tendency to move the policy towards that which is now increasingly commonplace in the West – essentially a policy of abortion on demand. I do not believe that was the initial intention of the UK legislation back in the late 1960s but the way the law was drafted has essentially allowed exactly that to be the outcome. Personally, I am dismayed at the way our society has blithely accepted the idea that under a positive banner of pro-choice, the lives of countless unborn babies have been ended. I just cannot reconcile how my profession has found a way to stand by and watch the slaughter of hundreds of thousands of lives. It is unconscionable. I do understand the arguments, of course. I realise that there is a risk from unsafe abortion practice and I realize that there may occasionally be a medical indication to terminate a pregnancy in order to preserve the life of the mother. I totally understand the policy behind contraception that groups like the Marie Stopes Foundation support but I cannot countenance or defend their active pro-abortion position. I am horrified that these baby killers are not only active here in Zambia (44,334 babies killed in 2018 under the Marie Stopes banner) but they are being supported to the tune of millions of dollars by democratically elected Western governments and multinational corporations. It looks like an unstoppable juggernaut. It is all very well to empower women and girls to take control of their futures. That is fine. However, it is a moral outrage to achieve that goal by poisoning or dismembering unborn babies whose future is sacrificed in the process. Whatever has happened to our sense of values? What about the principle of 'doing no harm?' In the UK there is a serious move to outlaw smacking of children after they are born. Isn't it bizarre that such a brutal and unnecessary practice cannot be tolerated yet it is considered perfectly legal and acceptable to rip an unborn child apart and so end his or her life? It seems to me that any sense of dignity or value in human life is simply ignored. I am equally horrified by the moves, once again, to support the killing off, of vulnerable, unwell or elderly people – I fear for a society that simply disposes of its inconvenient human problems. Whatever happened to the human race?

Obstetrics in the dark

Having had a rant about the awful business of baby killing, let's not dress it up with a clinically more acceptable term, I have now reasonable cause to moan about the personal cost of supporting the safe arrival of new human life. It was cost to my comfort – nothing more. I was called for two successive obstetric emergencies, both in the middle of the night and happily both with a successful outcome. One poor girl suffered what is known as a PPH - a post partum haemorrhage. Obstetrics can be a bloody business and when there is precious little blood available for transfusion it can quickly become a life-threatening emergency. In this case the afterbirth was incomplete and retained within the contracting uterus. It simply bled and bled and bled. A quick ultrasound scan confirmed that some placental remnants were retained and so a D&C was required. The team managed to source one miserable unit of blood for this new mother and even after that had been given her haemoglobin level was $3.8g/dL$. Mine is probably about $14-15g/dL$ and people would likely be transfused urgently in the UK with a level below about $8g/dL$. Despite decompensating and almost suffering circulatory collapse, we managed to get her blood volume up and keep things ticking over. Not long after crawling back into bed I had that awful sinking feeling when my phone rang again. This time a distressed baby – failing to progress; the call was for a Caesarian section. So I trudged back to the hospital where the team was more or less assembled. By that time the baby's head was almost visible and the lady was pushing like crazy. Happily the baby was born au naturel and I thankfully, yet again, made my return trip to bed.

Winker

Farmer's Day came around again as it does once a year in Zambia. It is essentially an excuse for a public holiday so no official hospital duties were scheduled. The result was that we really only had a morning's modest queue of patients to see. As usual, every specialty was represented. Maternity, gynaecology, urology, cardiology, paediatrics and surgery and lots of opportunity to use the ultrasound scanner to try to figure out what was what. We had thought of doing an elective section on a woman in the maternity unit because her twins were both lying in a transverse position at 37 weeks. They would be most likely undeliverable from that presentation. However, when

she was scanned this morning, the babies had turned into a breech position so she was left to her own devices. I was not off the hook however – another primigravida (woman in her first pregnancy) was failing to progress and showing signs of foetal distress so I sectioned her and delivered a baby boy who produced a one-eye open look of disdain at the whole process. As I looked at the photo I took of him later, I had second thoughts and

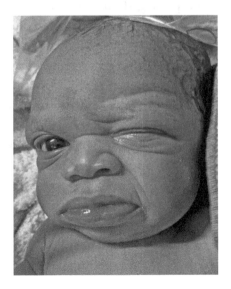

was left wondering whether he had a facial nerve palsy as a result of the delivery. I checked the following day and Dr. Ros agreed that indeed there was a facial palsy – hopefully it will be short lived.

James

For the last three weeks I have shared my house with James. He came out to join the maintenance team here and has worked like a Trojan doing all sorts of jobs - building, painting, tiling and plumbing. He was given the keys for a quad bike on the first day he spent in Chitokoloki and couldn't resist demonstrating a few 'doughnuts' in the sandy soil. Unfortunately, his lack of situational awareness was such that he chose to perform these stunts and high jinks outside the mission administrator's office. Needless to say, Mr. Hanna was not favourably impressed! The resulting frown spoke more than words and James got the message! Anyway, he has been good company. He has been the complete enthusiast about his work, about his free access to quad bikes and motorbikes although he has recently taken to bringing the motorbike into our kitchen overnight – presumably to prevent it from going astray. Having breakfast in an atmosphere contaminated by the smell of fuel is not the most pleasant experience. Like me, James shared the role of being a victim of the nocturnal attack dog! I was lying in bed one night and James had been out socialising. The dog went for him on his walk home. This being his second such experience he decided that the best approach would be to bark at the beast. All I could hear was the dog barking at James and James barking back at the dog with a very creditable imitation.

He is on the point of returning to his home in Holland to attend college. I did however take the opportunity of performing an unwitting social experiment. Last weekend our house worker, Thomas, was on leave for three days. We were left to our own devices. No one to wash our dishes, boil our water, do the laundry and generally tidy up. So as the weekend wore on, neither of us had been bothered to wash any dishes thus - reminiscent of student days, the kitchen sink began to pile up with crockery and cutlery. Well, on the Monday morning I was first to the kitchen for breakfast; got the porage going and used the last remaining clean bowl. I wondered how James would react. Would he wash one of the dirty bowls in the sink or would he resort to toast for breakfast? How would he face this stressful situation? Would he single-handedly restore my faith in Generation Z? From the adjacent room I heard him track to the cupboard for a bowl, vent his unspoken frustration at the lack of supply and then, clearly in a quandary, repair to the kitchen to consider his options. A few cupboards were opened - futile. You will be wondering about the result of this uncontrolled prospective trial - would he wash a bowl? Conclusion (albeit with a measure of extrapolation)? 18-year-old boys are not capable of washing any dishes even when hungry. He had a glass of water for breakfast and left for the day, apparently none the worse for his sad experience. Mercifully, Thomas appeared on cue and everything was set to rights later that morning.

David McAdam was determined that I clear as many of the major cases as possible before departing for the UK later in the week. Once I have gone he said, with feeling, "I'll have to do them all myself!" So David supervised the anaesthesia and, with the assistance of Hannah Dalton, a final year student, we did a couple of laparotomies, closed a stoma, did a nice thyroid lobectomy, a BTL and a brace of minor things. Some, we had to delay – again the lack of blood had paralysed us. We have no group O blood but we have three anaemic patients needing significant operations (gastrectomy, prostatectomy and hysterectomy) for whom it would be unwise to proceed without blood. All three patients were cross-matched as group O but their surgery will be delayed indefinitely until suitable supplies can be found.

Goodbye Chitokoloki

You become comfortable with familiar territory. For me, abdominal surgery in adults or adolescents presents no real concern. However, oral or indeed any head and neck surgery in a tiny infant is a different ball game altogether. We operated on a 4 month old baby with a big swelling under her tongue (a ranula) potentially quite an awkward procedure under ketamine. All went well although about 2 hours later the oxygen levels were low and she needed some resuscitation. It is truly amazing what can be accomplished without all the extra trappings of Western medicine; monitors, fancy scans, sophisticated laboratories and so on. All of these add a little but many of them are overused and unnecessary. In the low resource setting of Chitokoloki, we can provide simple safe care and while the range of confident decision making and diagnostic accuracy may be somewhat limited,

Note the operating light held together with sellotape and string!

and the range of therapeutic possibilities slightly reduced, safe care can still result. Just as we were winding up for the day, Dr Ros, our paediatrician, appeared from the clinic to show off two very impressive homemade crutches. We thought it a good excuse for a photo of the old clinicians!

I am sorry to be leaving this remarkable place and its remarkable people. Providing I am welcome, I would hope to return for future visits. My hope is that this book will convey something of the inequity in international healthcare provision and, not only that, I also hope that this account might inspire others to help in whatever way they can. It is an inspiring fact that the great bulk of healthcare in rural Africa is provided by faith-based services. I trust and pray that our experience has generated some interest, stimulated some to pray, or perhaps provoked some to give, whether time, energy, material resources or funds, that would all be positive. Every form of support has its place and will enable such a noble endeavour to continue, not just for the physical relief of suffering but for the spiritual healing that can only be found in the rescue plan outlined in the good news of the Lord Jesus Christ.

References

1. Meara JG, Leather AJM, Hagander L, Alkire BC, Alonso N, Ameh EA, et al. *Global Surgery 2030: evidence and solutions for achieving health, welfare, and economic development. The Lancet.* 2015 Aug;386(9993):569–624.

2. Turnbull A. *Chitokoloki: celebrating a century of the Lord's work in Northwestern Zambia.* Ontario, Canada L3K6A6: Gospel Folio Press; 2014.

3. Current Missionaries | *Chitokoloki Mission Hospital [Internet]. [cited 2020 Jan 27].* Available from: https://www.chitokoloki. com/missionaries1/missionaries/

4. Mission Flight Services - *Zambia [Internet]. Mission Flight Services. [cited 2020 Jan 20].* Available from: http://www. missionflightservices.com/operations/guesthouse/

5. Clarke I. *The Man with the Key Has Gone.* New Wine Press; 1998.

6. *Established Medical Charity Flying Medical Specialists around Zambia [Internet]. FlySpec. [cited 2020 Jan 21].* Available from: http:// www.flyspec.org/

7. *Brass Tacks | Serving Those Who Serve [Internet]. [cited 2020 Apr 1].* Available from: https://www.brass-tacks.org.uk/

8. Fergusson SJ, McKirdy MJ, Mulcahy E, Adams L. *Global Citizenship in the Scottish Health Service. The value of international volunteering.*

9. *Clarke's three laws. In: Wikipedia [Internet]. 2020 [cited 2020 Jan 25].* Available from: https://en.wikipedia.org/w/index.php?title=Clarke%27s_three_laws&oldid=935251242

10. Chama D, Ahmed Y, Baboo K, Halwindi H, Mulenga J. *Transfusion Transmissible Infections among Voluntary Blood Donors at the University Teaching Hospital, Lusaka, Zambia.* Med J Zambia. 2015;42(3):90–5.

Author's Note

How will the other half live?

Curiously, in the Spring of 2020, we find ourselves legally restricted by measures introduced to limit the spread of the SARS-CoV-2 pandemic. The viral illness associated with this can be devastating and some countries with sophisticated and well funded health systems have been overwhelmed by the severity of the viral pneumonia that develops in a proportion of infected individuals. Good quality data is still emerging and detailed figures for the prevalence and transmissibility of the virus remain matters for speculation and debate. The demand for critical care services and the risk of mortality are real enough as are the results of the economic standstill that has affected a huge section of the community.

In the UK it has been possible to rapidly scale up the response by sourcing additional equipment, supplies and staff as well as constructing numerous temporary hospitals around the country. In the UK there are some 28 doctors and 290 hospital beds per 10,000 of the population. Just think for a moment; how would people fare in a situation where there is only one doctor and 19 hospital beds per 10,000 of the population? Zambia, despite its mineral wealth remains a poor country with a GDP of nearly 27 billion US$ compared with

2.85 trillion US$ for the UK. According to the World Bank almost 60% of Zambians earned less than the international poverty line of $1.90 per day and the majority of the poor live in the rural areas.

If community transmission of coronavirus were to pick up speed in rural Zambia there would be limited time and limited resources to prepare a meaningful response. It would be essential to identify cases early, trace contacts and isolate them together with ensuring community engagement on hygiene and social distancing. It is hard to imagine how any of that could be effectively achieved in the African villages. Such health resources as there are would be quickly overwhelmed if Africa experienced the rapid acceleration of infection as occurred in Europe and the USA.

David McAdam wrote at the end of April 2020. *"We are kind of bracing ourselves for the worst yet hoping that with the Lord's mercy we might be spared the full onslaught that folk at home have encountered. We have two ventilators, maybe a couple of hundred good masks left over from the time of the Ebola scare, 10-20 visors and some scrubs plus a good supply of gloves, soap and disinfectants. Like the disciples we would be thinking "what are they amongst so many?" That, in essence, is our situation - one of watchful waiting for something that we know if it comes, will overwhelm us even more completely than in Europe or North America. In some ways it is a strange feeling with all the uncertainty, and yet we do have complete confidence in our God, that all is in his hands, as elsewhere in the world."*

It may be that in rural Africa, the effect of an age distribution that is much younger and a population that is less densely packed than in Western countries will have a mitigating effect. Perversely, the hospital may also be cushioned to some degree because of the lack of an effective ambulance or rescue service – it is common for people with major illnesses to take several weeks to get to Chitokoloki. People seriously affected by Covid-19 are unlikely to reach help in time.

What about the good news?

In several places in this book I have referred to the gospel – the good news which is at the heart of the Christian message. Perhaps the most concise description of the essence of this message was penned by an ancient writer in the first Century. He (the Apostle Paul) wrote to many friends around the ancient near East to encourage and inform fledgling Christian communities. Here is an example of his writing that brings into focus what this gospel is about and what is at stake. It is reproduced from the *English Standard Version* of the New Testament letter that Paul wrote to Christians in Rome.

Life in the Spirit

There is therefore now no condemnation for those who are in Christ Jesus. [2] For the law of the Spirit of life has set you free in Christ Jesus from the law of sin and death. [3] For God has done what the law, weakened by the flesh, could not do. By sending his own Son in the likeness of sinful flesh and for sin, he condemned sin in the flesh, [4] in order that the righteous requirement of the law might be fulfilled in us, who walk not according to the flesh but according to the Spirit. [5] For those who live according to the flesh set their minds on the things of the flesh, but those who live according to the Spirit set their minds on the things of the Spirit. [6] For to set the mind on the flesh is death, but to set the mind on the Spirit is life and peace. [7] For the mind that is set on the flesh is hostile to God, for it does not submit to God's law; indeed, it cannot. [8] Those who are in the flesh cannot please God.

[9] You, however, are not in the flesh but in the Spirit, if in fact the Spirit of God dwells in you. Anyone who does not have the Spirit of Christ does not belong to him. [10] But if Christ is in you, although the body is dead because of sin, the Spirit is life because of righteousness. [11] If the Spirit of him who raised Jesus from the dead dwells in you, he who raised Christ Jesus from the dead will also give life to your mortal bodies through his Spirit who dwells in you.

Heirs with Christ

[12] So then, brothers, we are debtors, not to the flesh, to live according to the flesh. [13] For if you live according to the flesh you will die, but if by the Spirit you put to death the deeds of the body, you will live. [14] For all who are led by the Spirit of God are sons of God. [15] For you did not receive the spirit of slavery to fall back into fear, but you have received the Spirit of adoption as sons, by whom we cry, "Abba! Father!" [16] The Spirit himself bears witness with our spirit that we are children of God, [17] and if children, then heirs—heirs of God and fellow heirs with Christ, provided we suffer with him in order that we may also be glorified with him.

Future Glory

[18] For I consider that the sufferings of this present time are not worth comparing with the glory that is to be revealed to us. [19] For the creation waits with eager longing for the revealing of the sons of God. [20] For the creation was subjected to futility, not willingly, but because of him who subjected it, in hope [21] that the creation itself will be set free from its

bondage to corruption and obtain the freedom of the glory of the children of God. [22] For we know that the whole creation has been groaning together in the pains of childbirth until now. [23] And not only the creation, but we ourselves, who have the firstfruits of the Spirit, groan inwardly as we wait eagerly for adoption as sons, the redemption of our bodies. [24] For in this hope we were saved. Now hope that is seen is not hope. For who hopes for what he sees? [25] But if we hope for what we do not see, we wait for it with patience.

[26] Likewise the Spirit helps us in our weakness. For we do not know what to pray for as we ought, but the Spirit himself intercedes for us with groanings too deep for words. [27] And he who searches hearts knows what is the mind of the Spirit, because the Spirit intercedes for the saints according to the will of God. [28] And we know that for those who love God all things work together for good, for those who are called according to his purpose. [29] For those whom he foreknew he also predestined to be conformed to the image of his Son, in order that he might be the firstborn among many brothers. [30] And those whom he predestined he also called, and those whom he called he also justified, and those whom he justified he also glorified.

God's Everlasting Love

[31] What then shall we say to these things? If God is for us, who can be against us? [32] He who did not spare his own Son but gave him up for us all, how will he not also with him graciously give us all things? [33] Who shall bring any charge against God's elect? It is God who justifies. [34] Who is to condemn? Christ Jesus is the one who died—more than that, who was raised—who is at the right hand of God, who indeed is interceding for us. [35] Who shall separate us from the love of Christ? Shall tribulation,

or distress, or persecution, or famine, or nakedness, or danger, or sword? [36] As it is written, "For your sake we are being killed all the day long; we are regarded as sheep to be slaughtered."

[37] No, in all these things we are more than conquerors through him who loved us. [38] For I am sure that neither death nor life, nor angels nor rulers, nor things present nor things to come, nor powers, [39] nor height nor depth, nor anything else in all creation, will be able to separate us from the love of God in Christ Jesus our Lord.

Finally

As a nation we have tried to honour the bravery and professionalism of NHS staff especially as they face the risks inherent in a global pandemic. Please remember the self-less and sacrificial attitude of our colleagues in Zambia. They have demonstrated a level of sacrifice and commitment, without the respite and background resources available in wealthy countries. They do certainly appreciate our support, whether by people praying for them, giving financially, sending excess medical supplies and equipment or even visiting to provide practical help.

All royalties from the sale of this book will be donated to the work of the Chitokoloki Mission Hospital.

If you would like to see the full colour versions of the images that have been reproduced here in monochrome, they are available on a web page for the book. This can be found at www.davidgalloway. co.uk where there is also some additional information.

David Galloway

May 2020